MADAME BOVARY

Borgo Press Books by GASTON BATY

Madame Bovary

MADAME BOVARY

A PLAY IN THREE ACTS

GASTON BATY

Adapted from the novel by Gustave Flaubert
Translated by Frank J. Morlock

THE BORGO PRESS
MMXII

MADAME BOVARY

FIRST BORGO PRESS EDITION

Published by Wildside Press LLC

www.wildsidebooks.com

DEDICATION

For Doctor Inger Rosner,
for saving my kidney,
and probably my life—
with sincere gratitude

CONTENTS

CAST OF CHARACTERS

Homais

Madame Lefrançois

Hippolyte

Binet

Abbé Bournisien

Léon

Serving Girl

Lheureux

Charles Bovary

Félicité

Emma Bovary

Madame Homais

Justin

The Beauties

Madame Caron

Rodolphe

Gérard

ACT I

SCENE 1

The Inn of the Golden Lion at Yonville L'Abbaye. An evening in March 1840.

The owner, Madame Lefrançois, comes and goes, bustling about. Mr. Homais warms his back standing before the large fireplace. Homais is all dressed in black, with green slippers and a velour bonnet with a gold tassel.

MADAME LEFRANÇOIS

Polyte! Polyte! Bring the twigs. Stop what you are doing, and bring up the brandy. Hurry up!

HIPPOLYTE

(from a distance) It's coming.

MADAME LEFRANÇOIS

If I only knew what dessert to offer the company you are expecting.

(Voices of two men singing in the adjoining room)

VOICES

So long as one can do it, toodaloo.
We will dance, falala.
So long as one can do it
We will drink,
Sing,
And love
Young wenches
So long as we can do it, toodaloooo.
We will dance, falalaaa.

MADAME LEFRANÇOIS

Good Heavens! There they are starting their racket all over.

HOMAIS

You entertain guests who do not breed melancholy. I heard them from my laboratory.

MADAME LEFRANÇOIS

The wagon drivers who brought the belongings of your physician. Imagine, Mr. Homais, that since then they've drunk eight pots of cider and had fifteen games of billiards.

VOICE

Double or nothing.

ANOTHER VOICE

Four-ball—corner pocket!

(Noise of billiard balls hitting each other. Applause.)

MADAME LEFRANÇOIS

Why, they're going to tear up my billiard table.

HOMAIS

Maybe that will get you to buy a new billiard table.

MADAME LEFRANÇOIS

A new billiard table!

HOMAIS

You must keep up with the times, Madame Lefrançois. Amateurs want straight pockets on the billiard table. And they have the idea, for example, of setting up a patriotic tournament for Poland, or the victims of the flood in Lyon.

MADAME LEFRANÇOIS

But it's so useful for me to arrange my wash! And in the hunting season I put up as many as six travelers!

HIPPOLYTE (enters with faggots on his shoulders; he limps)

Here's the brushwood.

MADAME LEFRANÇOIS

Put it on the kitchen fire.

VOICE

Seven!

ANOTHER VOICE

How many did you say?

FIRST VOICE

Seven. Let's see. Double strike and two balls.

SECOND VOICE

Seven.

HIPPOLYTE

I'm going to pull the wire.

HOMAIS

It's idle for you to say, Madame Lefrançois, that the infirmity with which this poor lad is afflicted doesn't trouble him in the exercise of his profession.

MADAME LEFRANÇOIS

It doesn't prevent him from running after girls.

HOMAIS

Not to mention his hideous limp, accompanied by a disgraceful balance in the lumbar region, is a thing that may keep travelers who are particularly squeamish from the Golden Lion.

MADAME LEFRANÇOIS

Do you truly think that, Mr. Homais? (six o'clock strikes on the large clock)

Six o'clock and the Swallow hasn't arrived yet. So long as Hivert hasn't broken a wheel, the way he did last month on the side of Bois-Guillame!

HOMAIS

Are you delaying your gentlemen's dinner by waiting for him?

MADAME LEFRANÇOIS

And what would Mr. Binet say! He has no equal for punctuality! And with that he's squeamish over nothing and difficult with cider. He sometimes comes at 7:30 and barely looks at what he eats.

HOMAIS

There's lots of difference between a notary clerk who received some education and an old rifleman become a tutor

(The clock chimes six times again. Binet enters: Prussian Blue coat falling straight around his body, grey pants, a leather cap on the top of his head held in place by cords.)

BINET

Servant.

MADAME LEFRANÇOIS

Good evening, Mr. Binet. Would you like me to set your place here?

BINET

No—as usual.

MADAME LEFRANÇOIS

There are some salesmen installed in the billiard room.

BINET

That's your business. Make them decamp.

MADAME LEFRANÇOIS

Fine. I'll go see.

BINET

Hold on! Cook that trout for me.

MADAME LEFRANÇOIS

Where'd you catch it?

BINET

In the Rieule. Near the mills.

(Madame Lefrançois leaves.)

HOMAIS

We're expecting the new doctor and his wife. Since our Polish refugee decamped, Yonville has been without a doctor.

BINET

And Yonville had great need of a doctor?

HOMAIS

Ah, I understand what you mean. No, question, I am here, and my great experiences in pharmacopeia renders me, indeed, as capable as another to give diagnoses and to battle illness with the weapons of science! But the law of 19 Ventose, Year 11, Article 1, forbids it, alas!—under the most severe penalties, the practice of medicine by any individual without specific diplomas, however capable they may be, besides their knowledge and their talent.

MADAME LEFRANÇOIS

(returning) Excuse, Mr. Binet, a short time more.

BINET

Eight minutes past six!

MADAME LEFRANÇOIS

Polyte!

HIPPLOYTE

Here I am!

MADAME LEFRANÇOIS

The cart belonging to the furniture removers remains by the large gate. Give them a hand to get it out of the way. The Hirondelle is capable of staving it in when it gets here. Do it quickly.

HIPPOLYTE

I'm on my way.

(Hippolyte and Madame Lefrançois leave.)

HOMAIS

His name's Charles Bovary.

BINET

Who?

HOMAIS

Our new doctor. He'd been established for the last four years in Tostes, and begun to find a niche there. But it seems the climate was pernicious to his wife, and that he must, without delay, change the air. He wrote me when he learned of the departure of this poor Yanoda. Between disciples of Aesculapius, one naturally renders these services to each other. On my side, I made inquiries as you may well imagine.

BINET (to Madame Lefrançois who crosses the room)

You'll butter my trout, won't you, and if you have a lemon—

HOMAIS

Between ourselves, he hasn't passed his doctorate.

BINET

Why?

HOMAIS

Mr. Bovary. He's a simple health officer. Still, he's said to be very capable. He'll bleed folks like nothing, and they say he has a fist from Hell for extracting teeth. As for his wife, she's a young woman from Ronault, the daughter of a big farmer by way of Vassonville. She received a beautiful education. She will give us a society.

BINET

What's that to me? I don't want to be part of their society.

HOMAIS

We're it only in the interest of your health, allow me to observe, Mr. Binet, that you ought not to refuse yourself all distractions.

BINET

Eh! These are not distractions that I lack. I angle fish and I twist the ends of napkins.

MADAME LEFRANÇOIS (returning)

This time the place is free. Whenever you like, Mr. Binet.

HOMAIS

Bon appétit!

BINET

Servant! (he leaves)

HOMAIS

He doesn't use his tongue for civilities!

MADAME LEFRANÇOIS

He never chats much. He came here last week. Two travelers with plenty to spare, full of wit, who told a bunch of jokes all evening till I was laughing till I cried—well, he remained there like a cod-fish without saying a word.

HOMAIS

Yes. No imagination, no witticisms, nothing of that which constitutes a man of society.

MADAME LEFRANÇOIS

Still, they say he has some means.

HOMAIS

In his profession it's possible. Ah, when a business man has considerable relations, when a jurisconsul, a doctor, a pharmacist become so absorbed that they become fantastic and churlish, I understand it. They are described in historical tracts. But at least they think of something.. Me, for example. How many times has it happened to me that looking for my pen on my desk to write a prescription, I found I had placed it behind my ear.

(The Abbé Bournisien, a fat man with a rubicund face under graying eyes, half opens the door and remains in the doorway. Homais turns toward the fire and pretends not to see him.)

MADAME LEFRANÇOIS

Ah, Monsieur Le Curé. What can I do to help you? Would you like something? A finger of liquor?

BOURNISIEN

You are indeed nice, Madame Lefrançois, but I never take anything between my meals. I thought that the Hirondelle must have arrived by now.

MADAME LEFRANÇOIS

It always does around this time. Certainly it's late; I don't know why.

BOURNISIEN

Hivert should be bringing me back my umbrella that I left the other day at the convent of Ernement. Would you be nice enough to have it sent to me in the evening?

MADAME LEFRANÇOIS

You can count on it. Polyte will bring it to you without fail. (Binet calls) I'm coming.

(The Curé leaves. Madame Lefrançois comes and goes to serve Binet)

HOMAIS

Well—what do you say to this inconvenience?

MADAME LEFRANÇOIS

What inconvenience?

HOMAIS

That refusal to accept refreshment. As if these priests were not the first to go on a spree when no one sees them. It's the most odious hypocrisy.

MADAME LEFRANÇOIS

Hypocrisy? No one is less of a hypocrite than our Curé. A fine brave man! And strong for all that. Last year he helped our folks go bring in the hay, and he carried as many as six bales at a time, he is so strong.

HOMAIS

Brave! In that case send your daughters to confession to characters with a temperament like that! As for me, if I were the government, I would bleed the priests once a month. Yes, Madame Lefrançois, every month, a large phlebotomy in the interests of the police and morals.

MADAME LEFRANÇOIS

Shut up, will you, Mr. Homais! You have no religion!

HOMAIS

I have a religion, my religion! I believe in the Supreme Being—whatever that may be doesn't concern me much—who placed us down here to fulfill our duties as citizen and father of a family.

(Léon enters. He's a well groomed young man with a gentle

manner, unsure of himself and a bit timid. His blond curly hair brushes his face. He does all this so he can look like the portrait of a Romantic.)

HOMAIS

What do you say about it, my young friend? A good God who lodges folks in the bellies of whales! It's not opposed to all the laws of physics? It won't suffice to demonstrate that priests stagnate in an ignorant sloth and force populations swallow it. With them?

LÉON

You know quite well, dear sir, that I don't meddle in politics.

A SERVING GIRL (putting her head in the door)

Have they brought the bonnets for Madame Caen?

MADAME LEFRANÇOIS

There's still hope. The Hirondelle hasn't got here yet.

HOMAIS

And what have you done good all this day?

LÉON

No big thing good, as usual I am bored with scratching stamped paper, then I get bored strolling the length of the river listening to the snoring of the tutor.

MADAME LEFRANÇOIS

I'm going to set your place with the company that Mr. Homais is expecting.

LÉON

Gladly, but I won't be indiscreet.

HIPPOLYTE (entering)

Here's a pot of cider for the travelers.

MADAME LEFRANÇOIS

Again!

HIPPOLYTE

They're installed under the shed in the old carriage lit by a candle, and went to play cards. (he leaves with his jug. Lheureux pushes through the door)

LHEUREUX

Very good day, ladies and gentlemen. They say that Hivert is late. No accident, I hope? I'm expecting a dispatch from Grand Sauvage.

MADAME LEFRANÇOIS

What brings you to chatter of an accident? The Hirondelle will get here in a minute or two.

LHEUREUX

I'm going to watch for it on the road. Excuse me, Madame. My respects, gentlemen.

(bowing as he leaves)

MADAME LEFRANÇOIS

Too polite to be honest!

HOMAIS

I am merely left to say that this cloth merchant will come to obtain the adjudication of cider for the hospital at Neufchatel.

MADAME LEFRANÇOIS

God, it's quite possible. He traffics in everything at the moment. An old peddler who had some stories not too clear. That doesn't prevent poor Cary putting his paws on this bird, and that one of these days he'll put a yellow placard on his door.

HIPPOLYTE

(returning) Now they need a half pint to whet them. (uproar of iron and bells and glasses shaking through the misty windows. One becomes aware of the arrival of the carriage. Lights run. Hipployte and Madame Lefrançois run outside with lanterns.)

VOICES

Attention. Watch out below. Watch out fatty! Keep back, little mother. Hohoo! Polignac! No accident. Polyte! Here! Pass the luggage without being told. Did you have a good trip? What did you get? Caught. Here: foot on the wheel. Do you have the dressmaker's box for Madame Caron? It's nothing, Madame Lefrançois. The dog of a little lady ran off. Polyte! Toss me the roll of shoes. The hampers. Here's another one. You are not badly loaded today. It's for days when we are not. Heavens, it's you, bad character! Here you are again in our country. As you see. Pay attention, will you, don't step on my corns. Pardon, excuse me. Do you have the box for Madame Caron? Patience, my beauty, you are young, you have time to wait. You are not the one who will cause us to quarrel. No—not those. Two packages sent express from Grand Sauvage to the address of Mr. Lheureux.

(Enter Charles and Félicité loaded down with packages.)

CHARLES

Put this down anywhere, and go back quickly to my wife.

HOMAIS

Doctor Bovary, no question?

CHARLES

Yes, Charles Bovary.

HOMAIS

I am Homais and your servant. Be welcome in Yonville. Did you have a good trip?

CHARLES

Yes, yes.—That is—my wife lost a little greyhound on the way that she really loved.

(he takes off his hat which he was wearing pushed down over his eyebrows. His round face, colored with feminine features and fat lips is further enlarged by short whiskers, and faded blonde hair cut straight over the face. He's all huddled in a large pilgrim cloak, large boots and gloves.)

VOICES

The box for Madame Caron. Yes, these two strong cadres, thanks! Polyte! Step on the ladder. Attention! Come drink a cup, one doesn't leave like that. The gray box up front; you've got to see it. Hivert! Something for me? Yes, Mr. Mayor. Watch out under the ladder! Just this little package, Mr. Mayor. Thanks. There's no more.

(At the same time, the conversation continues between Homais and Charles.)

CHARLES

She calls it Djali. He's a huntsman of the Marquis d'Andervilliers, who gave it to me when I eased him of a fluxion of the breast.

HOMAIS

It's truly regrettable that your arrival among us finds itself saddened by such a vexing incident.

CHARLES

It ran after the coach and suddenly could no longer be seen. The conductor stopped. He even turned back more than half a league with a great deal of complacency. But it's truly lost.

HOMAIS

And you say that Madame Bovary was moved to tears?

CHARLES

She's really going to miss Djali. When I wasn't home, my wife spent many hours talking to it as a confidante. That's what she just told me. I never suspected it.

VOICES

The box for Madame Caron. Here it is, my beauty, the box for Madame Caron. And at your service if you need anything. Polyte. There's nothing more under the tarpaulin.

(Enter Emma and Félicité. Lheureux follows them.)

CHARLES

Emma, come by the fire. Warm up. Allow me to present you to Mr. Homais—that I have not yet thanked for his letters.

HOMAIS

Very honored, Madame, and very happy that I've been able to render some services to the doctor.

(Emma responds with a sad smile and goes to the fireplace. She pulls her skirt up to her knees and puts her feet to the flame. She is tall, thin and supple. Her hair is pulled in two bands to each side. Her face is pale, but she has rosy cheeks, lips a bit plump, but large, superb eyes. Her hands are long, dry, with pointed nails.)

VOICES

Polyte. Here I am. Some coffee. And you know we are not teeto-
talers who take tea in tiny cups. Bring two pots and let them be
heavy. Minute.

(Noise of horses being unhitched.)

LHEUREUX

There's no need for Madame to give up hope of finding her dog.
My own father possessed a poodle, which, after twelve years
absence suddenly leapt on his back in the street one evening
when he went to dine in town.

CHARLES

You see!

HOMAIS

Mr. Lheureux is right. The *Journal de Rouen*, of which I
have the honor to be correspondent for the area of Bucher,
Neufchatel, and Yonville, recently cited a dog returned straight
from Constantinople to Paris.

LHEUREUX

And to envisage everything, if Madame's greyhound remains
lost, I am at Madame's disposition to promise her another of the
same breed.

EMMA

What's the use. One deception, more or less.

LHEUREUX

At your orders, Madame. Gentlemen, gentlemen. (he with-draws, bowing)

HOMAIS

Dinner will soon be ready. I dared to invite myself, my wife being absent, and we will have, if you like, a fourth guest, my young friend Léon Dupins, presently clerk at our notary's.

LÉON

Madame, Doctor.

CHARLES

Enchanted, sir.

HOMAIS

I will ask you one additional permission: that of wearing my Greek bonnet for fear of a head-cold.

CHARLES

Don't stay like this, Emma, sit down—rest.

EMMA

Yes, yes.

HOMAIS

Soon after dinner we will accompany you to your new home, and allow you to install yourselves there. Madame must indeed be weary? One is so shockingly jolted in our Hirondelle.

EMMA

It's true. But discomfort always amuses me. I love to change places.

LÉON

It's such a vexing thing to live nailed to the same place.

EMMA

Isn't it?

CHARLES

If you were like me, forced to be on horseback constantly—

LÉON

Why nothing is more agreeable it seems to me, if one can do it.

HOMAIS

All the same, the practice of medicine is not very hard in our country, for the condition of our roads permits the use of a carriage, and generally, the farmers pay well enough—being well healed.

EMMA

Do you at least have some walks in the vicinity?

LÉON

Oh, very few. There's a place called the Pasture on the height at the edge of the forest. Sometimes, on Sunday, I go there and stay there with a book, to watch the sunset.

HOMAIS

Aside from the ordinary cases of enteritis, bronchitis, and bilious diseases, we have a few fevers during the mowing season, but, in sum, nothing special to note if it's not much out of temper.

EMMA

I find nothing as admirable as sunsets, especially on the sea-shore.

LÉON

Ah, I adore the sea!

EMMA

Yes, the mind sails most liberally on this limitless stretch whose contemplation elevates the soul.

HOMAIS

You will find many prejudices to combat, Mr. Bovary. They still have recourse to novenas, to relics, to priests rather than coming naturally to a doctor or pharmacist.

LÉON

It's the same passing through the mountains. I have a cousin who traveled in Switzerland, who told me one cannot imagine the poetry of lakes, the charm of waterfalls, the gigantic effect of pine trees thrown across rivers or of huts suspended over precipices.

EMMA

Such spectacles must give ideas of infinity.

LÉON

Surely! And now I understand that musician who was in the habit of playing the piano before glaciers!

HOMAIS

To tell the truth, the climate isn't bad, and we number in the commune several nonagenarians. I myself have made some observations on the thermometer. In winter it goes down to four degrees, and in the hot sun reaches twenty-nine, thirty centi-grade, more or less—which gives fifty-four degrees Fahrenheit in English measurement.

CHARLES

Yes, yes, yes,

EMMA

You compose or play music?

LÉON

No, but I love it very much.

HOMAIS

Don't listen to him, Madame Bovary, he's pure modesty. He sings the guardian angel, believing it, but like an actor. We receive every other Sunday. Intimate little soirées. If you would honor us by being one of us, Mr. Léon would be forced to no longer hide his talent.

EMMA

Why, gladly, thanks. And what music do you prefer?

LÉON

German music—that which sets you dreaming.

EMMA

Do you know the Italians?

LÉON

Not yet, but I will see them next year when I live in Paris to finish my law degree.

EMMA

Paris!

HOMAIS

Still, Doctor, I must direct your attention the considerable presence of animals on the prairie adjoining the river. From which, exhalations of ammonia, that is to say, agote, hydrogen-oxygen—

EMMA

Paris!

HOMAIS

No, agote and hydrogen only—

MADAME LEFRANÇOIS

Come to dinner, ladies and gentlemen. And here's the charivari which resumes most beautifully. Excuse it. They are carriage drivers. They've been stuffing themselves since this morning at the expense of the Doctor.

CHARLES

What, at my expense?

MADAME LEFRANÇOIS

Listen to me then, if it's possible, my God.

VOICES

Life has some allures, give joy for them. Must it be spent, sadly, in regrets? Never! Never! Pleasure is French. Hey, youp, youp, youp, La, la, la, la.

CURTAIN

ACT I
SCENE 2

The main street in Yonville. A street lamp lights the shop window of Homais' pharmacy.

Hippolyte accompanies Félicité, carrying a lantern.

FÉLICITÉ

Go ahead to prepare the beds—that's easy to say. But I don't even know where to put my hand on the blankets in this flea-bag (motions)

HIPPOLYTE

Don't get upset. I will help you to find them. Is she bad, your boss?

FÉLICITÉ

It's not that she's bad, but with her one never knows on what foot to dance. One day, she'll spend hours talking in my kitchen as if she was with friends, the next day she'll scream she's going to throw me out because I didn't speak to her respectfully, or that I brought her a glass of water without putting it on a napkin.

HIPPOLYTE

It seems to mean that this must be an affected woman.

FÉLICITÉ

For example, she isn't alert. She leaves the keys on the buffet and never counts the sugar or the candles.

HIPPOLYTE

You must arrange for them to employ me to dig up the garden and groom the horse. The Lion of Gold allows me time each morning, and I don't ask a lot—for the mere end of seeing a pretty girl like you every day.

FÉLICITÉ

Wow! That's 'cause I'm from Montreuil where they make them all pretty.

HIPPOLYTE

You must take me to that land.

(He leaves. Charles and Homais go by.)

HOMAIS

The town hall was built on a design by an architect from Paris.

CHARLES

It's imposing for the locality.

HOMAIS

And here's the street lamp. I had elaborated a vast plan for
lighting daily, by agglomeration, but my colleagues on the
municipal council, still dominated by obfuscation, wouldn't
grant me the credits for a single street lamp, despite the argu-
ments I advanced for two hours by the clock. Still, they don't
light it when there's a clear moon.

CHARLES

Yes, yes, yes—

HOMAIS

My office.

CHARLES

Beautiful set-up.

HOMAIS

Your house is almost opposite. Down there where the serv
ant enters. You see your patients don't have a long journey to
execute your orders.

CHARLES

It has a nice approach from what I can make out.

HOMAIS

It presents the most suitable—principally for a doctor. It has a
gate which allows one to enter and leave without being seen.

(They pass. Léon and Emma enter.)

EMMA

Imagine—this is only the fourth time I'm going to sleep in a strange place. The day of my entry in the convent, that of my arrival in Tostes, and last Autumn at the château of Vaubyessard where we were invited to a ball. Each time it seems to me that a new phase of my life is opening up.

LÉON

I understand. One willingly understands that things cannot be found alike in different places.

EMMA

Yes, especially when one hasn't been happy.

(They leave in silence.)

CURTAIN

ACT I
SCENE 3

Homais' salon.

Sunday soirée. Léon is singing, Emma accompanies him. Homais and Charles are seated at a game table.

LÉON

Alas, cover up the over-proud soul,
I was able to believe in this love.
But your lying promise, Malvina,
Didn't last a day.
Toward his dwelling, joyous troupe
Direct your noisy echoes.
Name Fingal to the forgetful one,
Repeat to her my sad songs.

(Charles applauds)

HOMAIS

Hush! He's not finished.

LÉON

During long months of silence

At the depth of a vale, I waited for her.
I broke my bow and my lance,
I took my lute, I left.
Here's the cavernous gorge
Where your noisy echo died.
Flee, flee, joyous troupe
And leave me alone with my sad songs.

(Emma strikes a final chord and Homais applauds.)

HOMAIS

Didn't I tell you that he brings out the best of the romance like a tambourine or a Lablache?

LÉON

I wish that Mr. Homais were right, so as to be worthy of the accompanist.

CHARLES

Doesn't she play well? Imagine that she goes for months without opening her piano.

EMMA

When one cannot become an artist—

CHARLES

And her fingers run so quickly the whole length of the keyboard.

(Madame Homais enters, followed by Justin)

MADAME HOMAIS

Here's the mixture. Perhaps you'd prefer something else, but Homais wants to convert everybody to his mixtures. Put it down there, Justin.

HOMAIS

It's a decoction of tea, Tea Asiaticus. I introduced the custom into my home after the year of cholera. On the condition of not abusing it, you must see in it an exciting lightness, an agreeable taste, and with which I joined the happy influence of intellectual faculties. Allow me, to advise you, Madame, to sugar it with less parsimony. Pure sugar cane, Saccharum. I obtain it in the form of unrefined sugar and refine it myself in my laboratory.

EMMA

Thanks, thanks.

HOMAIS

Perhaps, Doctor, you'll observe to me that Holland and England where this beverage has spread to the point of being an almost daily custom among a large number of the inhabitants is present at the time the two countries when there is the greatest quarrel.

CHARLES

Really, Holland and England?

HOMAIS

But I'll reply to you that we can embellish this inconvenience by the addition of a sufficient quantity of milk, preferably not skim.—Allow me, Madame.

MADAME HOMAIS (to Justin who contemplates Emma.)

Well, are you going to remain standing there planted like a milestone? It's almost ten o'clock. Go to bed. And look to see if the children are not uncovered while they slept.

HOMAIS

One can add either rum from the Antilles or elixir de Garus, but that cannot be done without damaging the aroma.

(Justin leaves)

MADAME HOMAIS

He's a student in pharmacy, a distant cousin of Homais that we've taken in here from charity. Mr. Homais is good. Justin serves us, at the same time as a servant. He takes special care of the children.

EMMA

You have four, I believe?

LÉON

Napoléon, Franklin, Irma, and Athalia. Beautiful names, aren't they?

HOMAIS

I was looking for names evoking a great man, an illustrious deed, or a generous conception. Napoléon represents glory, and Franklin, liberty. Irma, was chosen, I admit, from a concession to fashion, but Athalia is a homage to the most immortal masterpiece of the French stage.

LÉON

Eh, Mr. Homais, a play in which God is the main character! So you are not quite so much an enemy of the priests?

HOMAIS

My young friend, my philosophic convictions don't interfere with my artistic admiration, and the thinker in me doesn't suffocate the man of feeling.

MADAME HOMAIS

In any case, Athalia is a demon. Ah, Madame, what Christian-torment these children are! With them one is at the mercy of a thoughtless action, thus I beware myself, you can believe me. In our home the knives are never sharpened, the floors are never waxed, all the windows have grills, and until they're at least four, I make our little ones wear cushioning pads around their heads.

HOMAIS

I can do nothing but approve of that, Madame Homais. A simple concussion can have formidable results for the intellectual organs. You intend then to make them from the Caribes or the Botocudos?—Another cup, dear Madame?

EMMA

Thanks.

HOMAIS

And you, Mr. Léon?

LÉON

I thank you all the same.

(The bell, suspended from a pendulum rings ten times.)

HOMAIS

Ten o'clock. What would you say now, Doctor, to a game of dominoes in three hundreds?

CHARLES

That would revive me. When I was a medical student in Rouen, I developed a passion for dominoes. How many courses didn't it make me fail. It was my sole fantasy.

HOMAIS

It's necessary that youth pass.

MADAME HOMAIS

You're getting settled in as you like?

EMMA

Many things that I wanted to keep for memory were abandoned or lost in transport.

CHARLES

It's correct to say that two moves are as bad as a fire. And what expenses moving necessitates.

MADAME HOMAIS

If I can be useful to you, dispose of me quite freely. I need to tell you when I get provisions. Here, like everywhere, you find the same thing at the best price at different places. For example, your supply of butter—

EMMA

I will send Félicité to you for all that—if you really would. She'll understand better than I will.

MADAME HOMAIS

Ah, as for the garden.

EMMA

I don't concern myself with gardens.

CHARLES

That's very regrettable, since it involves exercise. But my wife prefers to read in her room.

MADAME HOMAIS

All day long?

HOMAIS

If Madame will do me the honor of using it, I have at her disposal a library composed of the best authors, Voltaire, Delille, Pigault-Lebrun—the Echo of Feuilletons.

EMMA

I've read all that.

JUSTIN

(entering timidly) Madame—

CHARLES

Your play.

JUSTIN

Athalia

MADAME HOMAIS

Athalia has caught the colic again. Excuse me. Poor sweetie! I need to go to her.

HOMAIS

Two and a half ounces of farina of flax, prepared as a poultice, and watered with three drops of laudanum. (Madame Homais leaves with Justin) Double six.

LÉON

I could give you the address of a reading room in Rouen where I subscribe myself. Hivert carries the volumes back and forth. Here, far from the world, it's my sole distraction.

CHARLES

Four.

HOMAIS

Spades.

LÉON

What could be nicer than to be next to the fireplace in an evening with a book while the wind beats at the window panes—?

EMMA

Yes.

LÉON

The hours pass. One walks motionless in the country that one thinks to see. One recognizes in the corner of a page vague ideas that one had, and one has forgotten. It's like a dark image which comes back from a distance.

EMMA

I've experienced that.

LÉON

It's especially the poets that I love. I find verse more tender than prose, and they are better at making one cry.

EMMA

Still, it's living in the long run. Now, on the contrary, I adore long stories that introduce fear. I detest common heroes, and temperate feelings, as there are in Nature.

LÉON

No question. What's the use of imagining if what one imagines is not better than life?

EMMA

I remember—I was twelve when I read Paul and Virginia, and I dreamed and dreamed.

A WOMAN'S VOICE

Dreamed.

(While someone breathes and causes flickering of the lamplight, invisible beings answer in a muffled way. Emma doesn't seem to hear the voices and doesn't interrupt her conversation with Léon; from a distance one of the real phrases of her conversation interrupts the phantasmagoric murmuring.)

VOICES

The little Bamboo hut.
The Negro Domingo.
The dog, Fido.

The good little brother who's going to find red fruits for you in the big trees—as tall as clocks, or who runs with naked feet on the sand—to bring you a bird's nest.

EMMA

And what emotion when I discovered Walter Scott.

VOICES

Dwellings
Guard rooms.
Minstrels.

EMMA

It was a fine time. I believed I lived those adventures, and palpitated under the costumes of characters.

VOICES

We've all been the young girl in a white dress who pecked at a dove through the bars of a gothic cage—

Or she who, smiling and head bowed, pulls off the painted petals of a flower.

In the darkest part of the forest, where they kill the postilions of all relays, we fainted in an abandoned pavilion. Janissaries presented us, captive and naked to Sultans who smoked narghile water pipes beneath trellises. Knights risked their lives to clasp us in their arms and we fainted.

EMMA

He has words like magic which soothe the depths of the soul with unexpected sweetness.

VOICES

Lagoons, gondoliers.
Rafts, in the moonlight.
Melancholy ruins.
Songs of dying swains.

Falling leaves.

(The clock strikes twelve. Light returns. Charles and Homais have finished their game of dominoes, and are dozing. Emma and Léon continue to speak in low voices.)

EMMA

Midnight already!

LÉON

Look, they are dozing.

EMMA

Hush!

LÉON

Hush! So then, after this morning, your father placed you in a pension with the Ursulines of Rouen. And then?

EMMA

What to say! I loved the convent. Its tepid, the smell of incense. I was so pure. Can you imagine that when I went to confession I invented little sins so as to remain longer on my knees in the shade?

I had many friends among my companions. We promised to write each other, but we didn't continue for very long. My life is very different from theirs. What became of them, those whose coats filled the courtyard the day of the Fest of God, or for the distribution of prizes? They are rich, elegant and admired. Doubtless they love and are loved. For them the delicacy of luxury, of the happiness of dreams that are accomplished, the nobility of an idea. I imagine them, when they go to the theater in their box seats, under shining lights. They greet one another with a bow of their heads, with headbands gently bulging. Flowers hang from their necks. Pearls roll on their shoulders, They wave their fans. They smell their bouquets to hide their smiles, they—

(in measure to her words the stage is lit up and the Beauties appear as they are described—then shadow invades Homais' salon, except for the illuminated face of Emma.)

THE BEAUTIES

Emma!
Emma, you are one of us! You are really worth as much as all
    those who live happily.
Your waist is less thick, and your manners less plebian than
    duchesses.
Listen to us, Emma.
We are bringing you the dream, the great romantic dream.
On it we have modeled our lives.
On it, you can model yours.
To live, one must dream one's life.
Choose among the images of yourself.
Choose to be haughty and wild,
Faithfull without love, and virtuous through pride.
Savor the sensuality of being stronger than your desires.
Aspire to the vertigo of sacrifice and isolation.
Be the unreachable vine, heavy with grapes that none can press.
And if your pride is not powerful enough,
And if the need to love bursts in your breast,
Go strengthen yourself in God,
Go cast your love to God.
In the cold shadow of gothic naves,
Where tones do not echo in the silence,
Rush to the rendezvous with your celestial fiancée!

Passionate!—Be the lamp that consumes itself on vigil in the
    sanctuary.
Languishing—be the sheep whose good shepherd takes it on his
    shoulders.
Gorged with disgust for this world, and scorn for its inhabitants,
Raise yourself ever higher.
We are bringing you the liberating dream,
Stretch out your hands, take it!

(Abruptly, the voices are silent.)

FELICITY'S VOICE

Madame!

(Suddenly the room of the Bovary's appears.)

CURTAIN

ACT I

SCENE 4

A ground floor room where one stays or eats. The walls are hung with yellow silk paper, and curtains of white muslin over the windows. The mirror over the chimney reflects a hanging of the head of Hippocrates between two bouquets beneath a globe. There's a round table with a green cloth, an old lamp, a barometer, a clock, an armchair à la Voltaire, and straw chairs. It's April at sunset.

FÉLICITÉ

Madame, here's the dish cloths.

EMMA (stretching her hands)

Let me have them.

FÉLICITÉ

Madame Rollet came to do the wash. But we are going to need ashes. Perhaps, I should go ask them of Madame Homais.

EMMA

If you like.

FÉLICITÉ

And this evening? How many should I set for?

EMMA

You know quite well.

FÉLICITÉ

Mr. Léon is staying to dinner?

EMMA

Yes, the Doctor invited him. You will fold the napkins into a priest's bonnet, the way I've shown you. And then you must make a Souvaroff.

FÉLICITÉ

What's that?

EMMA

A pot of pear Jell-O turned over on a plate topped with vanilla cream.

FÉLICITÉ

Ah, right.—Why do they call it—what you called it?

EMMA

Souvaroff. It's a Russian name.

FÉLICITÉ

There's still another matter, Madame.

EMMA

Well, say it.

FÉLICITÉ

Polyte. Madame recalls that he grooms the horse every morning. He hasn't been paid for two weeks.

EMMA

Truly?

FÉLICITÉ

He is in my kitchen.

EMMA

I don't have the money now. Remind me to speak to the Doctor tonight.

(a bell rings)

Go, quickly to open. If it's Mr. Léon—no, go.

(Félicité leaves. Emma looks for a moment in the mirror, sits down, takes a washcloth and begins to work.)

FÉLICITÉ

It's Mr. Lheureux. He says he wants the favor of being received by Madame.

EMMA (throwing away the cloth)

Show him in.

(Lheureux enters carrying a big green box.)

LHEUREUX

Madame will indeed excuse my boldness in presenting myself thus in her home. For a month since Doctor Bovary has been in Yonville, I was hoping every day that Madame would come to honor me with her confidence.

EMMA

It's that I don't need anything, Mr. Lheureux.

LHEUREUX

You always need something pretty. I'm well aware that a poor shop like mine isn't made to attract an elegant lady. But Madame has only to command. I will undertake to furnish you with whatever you want, be it lingerie, hats, novelties. I go to the city regularly, four times a month, to the Three Brothers or the Golden Ball. Those gentlemen know me like their old clothes. Today, I merely came to show Madame, in passing, different articles I can dispose of.

EMMA

Thanks, I have all I need.

LHEUREUX

You can always glance over it, embroidered collars, feathers, Muslim attached to Brussels lace. Isn't this mixture of crochet and relief work original? Another in braid? No?

EMMA

No.

LHEUREUX

It's stitched. Simple and very easy to wear. Still the placement of festoons gives it lots of chic. I can procure assorted sleeves for it. But here's better affectation. The novelty of the season. You won't see anything else this year. And better yet, necktie Margot. It's a model from the house of Limart, rue Rambuteau, in Paris.

EMMA

Let me see.

LHEUREUX

Just try it, Madame. Allow me. Taffeta embroidered the old way. Is it not becoming? It suffices to wear it on a dress of poplin or wool. For an evening party, for a spectacle, for a fest—the scarf can fall back over your back and follow the movement of your bare neck.

EMMA

Decidedly, no. I thank you again.

LHEUREUX

Here are three Algerian scarves. A very rare opportunity. They are authentic and come directly from that country. One of my nephews served in the army under General Lamericière. How supple, brilliant, nuanced! And that's not all. If you like curiosities, I have—

EMMA

The scarves are pretty.

LHEUREUX

Admire how the gold is interwoven with the silk, it's the secret of Moorish material.

EMMA

How much do they cost?

LHEUREUX

A pittance.

EMMA

But still?

LHEUREUX

A pittance. Besides, there's no rush. We are not Jews.

EMMA

I thank you again, Mr. Lheureux. But what would I do with

them? An honest woman has no use for Algerian scarves.

LHEUREUX

Right, right. As Madame pleases. I am sure that we will understand each other. With ladies, I always work things out. Except
with my wife. Don't let it be money that worries you. I'd rather
give it to you than let you lack it. Why, yes, I won't have to go
far to find you. At your service.—You really don't want me to
leave you the scarves?

EMMA

Truly, no. *Au revoir*, Mr. Lheureux.

LHEUREUX

In the end, *au revoir*, Madame Bovary. At your disposal. Your
very humble servant.

(he leaves.)

EMMA

How prudent I was, Félicité.

FÉLICITÉ

Madame.

EMMA

You need to go light the fire. Evenings are still chilly.

FÉLICITÉ

April is the most treacherous month. I have the pot on in the kitchen.

(she leaves)

EMMA

It must already be Summer in Algiers.

(Félicité returns and sets fire to the faggots.)

Did the postman come?

FÉLICITÉ

Yes, Madame, he had nothing for us.

EMMA

Do you think it will rain tomorrow? The skies are all grey on the side of Neufschatel.

FÉLICITÉ

It rained at Saint-Gervais, therefore—

EMMA

Now, the horses are going to drink and the Angelus hasn't sounded.

FÉLICITÉ

Lestiboudois is no longer on time; he comes when he pleases, so as not to take from his work.

EMMA

The school master is strolling with the hatter. What can they be talking about every day? And Justin is still at the window looking this way. Does he know what Mr. Homais intends? He thinks that Justin comes so often because he's in love with you.

FÉLICITÉ

I don't believe that, Madame.

EMMA

Pay attention, Félicité. If it were true, you would need to apply yourself to discourage that little kid. It's a duty when one is honest.

FÉLICITÉ

Yes, Madame.

EMMA

Madame Tuvache and her daughter are coming from Madame Caron's. How old can Madame Tuvache, be?

FÉLICITÉ

I don't know.

EMMA

And then, what's it matter? Ah—go open, quickly, Félicité. No. Wait.

(she sits down and leans on her elbows.. Bell rings.)

Go quickly!

(Léon enters)

LÉON

My respects, Madame.

EMMA

Good evening.

LÉON

I allowed myself to come as soon as the office closed.

EMMA

My husband hasn't returned yet. But sit down, I beg you. And excuse me for not interrupting my work. There are so many things to do in a house.

LÉON

Don't disturb yourself for me. It's very delightful for me to remain near you, watching you ply your needle. I often think—

EMMA

Yipes! It's nothing. I just stuck myself.—You were saying.

LÉON

I have to go to Rouen one of these days. Your music subscription has ended, should I renew it?

EMMA

No.

LÉON

Why?

EMMA

Because.

LÉON

You actually intend to abandon it?

EMMA

Music? Don't I have many duties which are more important?

LÉON

With talent like yours—

EMMA

I'm worried because my husband is late. He's so devoted to his patients that he doesn't know the time to leave them.

LÉON

I hear everyone praising him.

EMMA

At first he was scared because patients didn't come. Now, I'm going to complain they come too much.

LÉON

Don't complain. They sing his praises not only because he's an excellent doctor, but because he is nice to children, that he never goes to a cabaret, that he—

EMMA

Yes, yes. He's a brave man.

(Félicité comes in to light the lamp. Félicité brings in the doctor's slippers and warms them up at the fire.)

FÉLICITÉ

His slippers.

EMMA

Yes, they're on the rug I knitted for him.

FÉLICITÉ

Fine.

(Félicité leaves.)

LÉON

While you sew, would you like me to continue reading from your fashion journal, like the other evening?

EMMA

Thanks. I've decided to no longer take either the Corbeille or the Sylphe de Salons. What to do with them, I ask you? I will no longer go to the ball, and don't have to be "elegant," as Mr. Lheureux puts it.

LÉON

For a little you would speak like our good Madame Homais. "But I don't take an interest in dressing because I've never been able to put on a corset."

EMMA

Don't laugh. She's the one who is right. A mother doesn't bother herself about frivolities.

(Félicité brings slippers and leaves.)

LÉON

I swore to speak to you this evening.

EMMA

Would you please pass me another napkin? Thanks.

LÉON

Madame.

EMMA

Well, speak.

LÉON

There's such peace, such calm around you.

EMMA

Such calm? Yes, perhaps it's not happiness, but it's something that resembles it a bit.

LÉON

And you are satisfied?

EMMA

Me? I have to be.

LÉON

You weren't made for this.

EMMA

What do you know about it?

LÉON

Before your arrival, I, too, knew it, this calm. And each morning I hoped for the day something would deliver me from it, Like a sailor in distress looking for a sail on the sea.

EMMA

A sail.

LÉON

A sloop is a ship with triple decks, loaded with anguish or joys, no matter which—so long as it comes.

EMMA

Mr. Léon, be good enough to fix the lamp—it's flickering.

LÉON

You came.

EMMA

A little bit more. Thanks. You speak like a child. Perhaps, I would have said some things, formerly. But when years pass, file by, always the same, without bringing anything—

LÉON

If you would listen to me—

EMMA

As for me—nothing will happen to me. God wanted it. May His will be done! And I don't complain. I am not unhappy.

FÉLICITÉ

Here's the Doctor.

(Charles enters.)

EMMA

Good evening, my friend.

CHARLES

Good evening, my little kitty-cat.

EMMA

You really made yourself wait.

CHARLES

Hello, Mr. Léon.

EMMA

I was beginning to get worried.

CHARLES

But it's no later than usual. I always return the same time. I was in town at Tastermain, at Langlois—the little one is safe now, then I went to Buchy to bleed old man Courvier and at Saint Laurent meadows for Mistress Prentout.

EMMA

I'm going to write them down right away.

CHARLES

Imagine—my wife now insists on listing my visits and declares it was she who sent patients their notes. They are receiving letters—better written notes than mine—It's nice to be at home!

EMMA

I've prepared your slippers.

CHARLES

Oh! How nice you are to think of such things. But why, exactly, tonight?

EMMA

Mr. Léon will allow you to change boots.

LÉON

Look!

CHARLES

My wife always reproaches me for big boots with their folds in the instep. Still, it's good enough for the country.

EMMA

Félicité, you can set the table.

FÉLICITÉ'S VOICE (off stage)

Fine, Madame.

CHARLES

I am sure that you will still be talking of your readings. How can you absorb so many books like that? As for me, I only receive The Medical Ruche to keep up to date, and I try to read a little of it every evening. But, no sooner have I stuck my nose in it than I doze off. It's stronger than I am.

EMMA

My husband has no ambition.

LÉON

You are the very image of happiness.

CHARLES

It's true we've nothing to complain of. Right, Emma?

CURTAIN

ACT I

SCENE 5

Before the door of the Church, A late afternoon in May.

Sharp voices intone a song. Emma stops to listen. Abbé Bournisien enters.

VOICES

One day. I'll go to heaven, to heaven, to heaven.
I'll go there one day.
In heaven, in its country
Yes, I'll go see Mary
My joy and my love.
One day—I'll go to heaven, to heaven, to heaven.

EMMA

Monsieur Le Curé.

BOURNISIEN

Oh, Madame Bovary, excuse me, I didn't see you. That's because—be it said without offense—I'm not used to meeting you in my church.

EMMA

You will see me often now. Devotion alone can save me.

BOURNISIEN

Indeed, it is necessary to salvation.

EMMA

No matter what devotion—so long as it curbs my soul, and my entire life vanishes in it.

BOURNISIEN

That's a fine thought. Still, one mustn't exaggerate. When you say no matter what devotion—

THE SINGERS

One day I'll go to see it.
Heaven's Gate.
A sweet hand will carry me
To eternal rest.

BOURNISIEN

Those young girls are waiting for me, for the for the exercise of the month of May.

EMMA

I recognize the song. We sang it in the convent. I was listening when you got here. And it seemed to me I again saw huge chandeliers around the altar, vases full of flowers, and the sweet face of the Holy Virgin among the bluish whirlwinds of incense that were rising.

BOURNISIEN

That's because these Ursuline ladies are sufficiently well off to pay for incense of the first quality. In our poor parishes, we must be satisfied with a mixture in which there's also a lot of resin. The smoke is not as blue.

SINGERS

One day I'll go to heaven, to heaven, to heaven!

EMMA

It was a good time. I ought to have become a nun.

BOURNISIEN

If the Lord didn't call you, it's because he destined you for marriage. One can be sanctified in all situations. But, forgive me, I must get back to the children. And I haven't even asked you if you are well.

EMMA

Oh, I'm ill.

BOURNISIEN

Well, me, too. These first heats soften you to an astonishing degree. We were born to suffer as Saint Paul said.

EMMA

I feel myself indolent and abandoned like a bird's feather blown by the storm.

BOURNISIEN

For goodness sakes! And what does Mr. Bovary think about it?

EMMA

He—

BOURNISIEN

He doesn't prescribe anything for you.

EMMA

There are no remedies on earth which will help me.

SINGERS

One day I will go see.
I will join the angels too
To sing his praise.
I will go see Him one day.

BOURNISIEN

The Doctor himself, how is he? Still very busy no doubt? We are certainly the two persons of the Parish who have the most to do. But he's a doctor of bodies, as I am of souls. (he laughs)

EMMA

Yes, you assuage all misfortunes, right?

BOURNISIEN

Don't speak to me of them, Madame Bovary! This morning I had to go to Bas-Diauville for a bloated cow. They thought it was a fate. These farmers are really to be pitied.

EMMA

There are others, too.

BOURNISIEN

Assuredly. The workers in the towns, for example.

EMMA

It's not them.

BOURNISIEN

Yes, indeed. I've known poor mothers of families who even lack bread.

EMMA

But those, Monsieur Le Curé, who ought to have bread and don't have—

BOURNISIEN

Fire in winter?

EMMA

Eh, what difference does it make?

BOURNISIEN

What do you mean? What difference does it make! It seems to me that when one has enough heat, enough to eat—

EMMA

My God! My God!

BOURNISIEN

You find that irritating. Digestion, no doubt? You must go home, Madame Bovary, and drink a glass of cold water with balm.

EMMA

Why?

BOURNISIEN

I thought that a dizziness had seized you. But, don't you have something to ask of me?

EMMA

Nothing, nothing—

SINGERS

One day I'm going to heaven, to heaven, to heaven—

BOURNISIEN

This time is great weather. Wouldn't you like to be one of us during Mary's month? You were telling me just now—

EMMA

Too late.

BOURNISIEN

Barely six o'clock. But, if your household reclaims you, the duties of your situation always come first. Best of health, Madame. My respects to your husband, the Doctor.

(He goes back into the Church. Emma leaves.)

SINGERS

I will go to see it one day.
It's the sacred hope
Which calms all suffering,
Of a son of his love.
I will go one day to see heaven, to heaven, to heaven, to heaven.

CURTAIN

ACT I
SCENE 6

The Bovary home. A morning in June. Emma is at the window.

FÉLICITÉ

Madame, it's Justin. He's come running. He wants to see you with all his strength. It was in vain for me to tell him—

EMMA

Fine. Let him come in.

(Félicité lets Justin in and leaves.)

JUSTIN

Ah, Madame.

EMMA

What's wrong, Justin?

JUSTIN

This is it, madame. Just now I was in the laboratory; I heard someone enter the Pharmacy and speak with Mr. Homais. It was—it was Mr. Léon.

EMMA

Yes—I saw him go by. Well?

JUSTIN

He said he was leaving this morning.

EMMA

He's going to Rouen?

JUSTIN

No—to Paris.

EMMA

To Paris. For how long?

JUSTIN

Forever.

EMMA

What do you mean?

JUSTIN

He's going right away.

EMMA

And then?

JUSTIN

Then I thought that Mr. Homais would soon bring you news and that Mr. Léon was going to come. But that it would be better you knew in advance.

EMMA

Why would it be better?

JUSTIN

I thought it was the right thing. I ask your pardon.

EMMA

Your boss. Escape by way of the court, Justin. Thanks.

(Justin leaves. Emma hides her face in her hands, then at the sound of the bell, straightens up and seems to be reading calmly when Homais enters.)

HOMAIS

My respects. You are *au courant* of the event?

EMMA

What event?

HOMAIS

Our young man is leaving.

EMMA

What young man is that?

HOMAIS

Why, Léon. We just now put him in a carriage.

EMMA

He's going to Rouen?

HOMAIS

No, to Paris.

EMMA

Really? Is he planning to stay there long?

HOMAIS

He's going to settle in there, imagine!

EMMA

That's a surprise.

HOMAIS

You can say that. You're a woman with a head, Madame Bovary. But my wife, who is more sensitive than you, is overwhelmed.

EMMA

How did it happen?

HOMAIS

It was always a question of his going to Paris to finish his law degree. A plan of which he spoke often, prior to your arrival. Recently, one might think he had renounced them. Quite to the contrary. He made his preparations in secret. If he kept us all in ignorance of the outcome, it's because he had at heart, no question, the idea of shortening as much as possible the emotion of goodbyes. Don't you think so?

EMMA

No question.

HOMAIS

To tell the truth, I hadn't failed to notice a certain melancholy in him, I would even say a certain sadness for the last several weeks. Madame Lefrançois had told me that he no longer had an appetite and left food on his plate. But I imagined some young man's story. Myself, when I was his age. The young guy will be like a fish out of water in the capital. Fine parties at the home of the Rector. Masked balls! Champagne! He won't miss Yonville very long, I assure you.

EMMA

Yes, he'll forget quickly.

HOMAIS

He'll need to follow the others at the risk of passing for a Jesuit.

You cannot imagine the lives these jokers lead in the Latin Quarter with the grisettes.

(Enter Justin)

JUSTIN

Sir.

HOMAIS

Not a moment's respite!

JUSTIN

They need you right away to prepare a chicken milk.

HOMAIS

A chicken milk! Always at the chain-gang. I cannot leave for a moment. It's necessary to work like a horse, to sweat blood and water! Till soon, Madame Bovary.

(he leaves)

JUSTIN

Here's Mr. Léon.

HOMAIS

(returning)

By the way, I convoked my cider merchant. It's a business all taken care of. I will see to it myself that the cask be well placed in the wine cellar.

EMMA

Yes, yes.

JUSTIN

Sir.

HOMAIS

What a necklace of misery!

(Justin and Homais leave. Emma is on her feet, motionless and tense, awaiting Léon. Léon enters.)

LÉON

I came—

EMMA

I know

LÉON

The Doctor isn't here.

EMMA

He's making his visits.

LÉON

You will indeed give him my goodbyes, and thank him for his kindness.

EMMA

I shan't fail. It's going to rain. Do you have a cloak?

LÉON

Yes.

EMMA

At our first meeting, you told me of what your life would be in Paris. Are you still planning on taking guitar lessons?

LÉON

Yes.

EMMA

And to place on your chimney a death's head with two foils in a long chain.

LÉON

Listen to me, I beg you.

EMMA

What's the use?

LÉON

It's important that you know what you mean to me. When you came into my life—

EMMA

I didn't come into it.

LÉON

I am clumsy. What I mean is—

EMMA

Talk. Keep talking.

LÉON

I will keep an imperishable memory of days spent with you, I will ceaselessly see your pale cheeks, your warped headbands, your big eyes, your bird-like gait. It's a very profound feeling, and it ought not to offend you.

EMMA

You imagined—

LÉON

You must forgive me. I understand what an exceptional human being you are. I read on your face the imprint of a sublime destiny. When I contemplated you, so virtuous, so pure, so sad, and so calm, all at the same time, I repented of having failed to love you like a woman.

EMMA

You failed—?

LÉON

But, it's over. I will venerate you like a saint. You soar above me, outside of flesh, outside of life—Will you pardon me for not having recognized it right away?

EMMA

Yes.

LÉON

Will you give me your hand?

EMMA

Here it is.

LÉON

Good bye, goodbye.

EMMA

Yes, goodbye. Leave!

(straight and icy she watches him leave; waits a little bit, then when the street door shuts, she starts laughing crazily.)

A saint! A saint! Now you're satisfied, I hope! That virtue which promised to repress love if it dared to come! Love didn't even dare! That's what it is to be proud.

(she collapses, sobbing)

It's fine, huh! isolation, duty, sacrifice 1 It's vain—a heart that shivers and a useless body! The mystic rose. Idiot!

FÉLICITÉ (running in at the noise)

What is it, Madame? Madame!

EMMA

Leave me alone, it's nothing.

FÉLICITÉ

I'm going to find the Doctor.

EMMA

No. Not worth the trouble. Just nerves. It's already over, you see.

FÉLICITÉ

Saving your respect, you are worn out, Madame, from staying in your armchair with your books. I don't know what you can be thinking and rehashing about, like this, for hours at a time, without moving, your arms and legs like a wooden saint.

(Emma begins to bawl again.)

Your nerves are knotted, that's certain. Why not tell the Doctor about it?

EMMA

I don't want to. I forbid you to speak to him about it.

FÉLICITÉ

Fine, Madame, fine. Still—

EMMA

Shut up!

FÉLICITÉ

You are exactly like the daughter of old man Guerin, the fisherman from Pollet. She was so sad that to see her standing in the doorway of her house had the effect on you of seeing a burial flag. The doctors couldn't do a thing, nor the priests, When it took her hard, she would go all alone to the shore and weep on the shingle. It seemed that it passed after her marriage.

EMMA

As for me, it's after marriage that this came to me.

(an organ plays a waltz.)

Oh! That music, Make it stop!

FÉLICITÉ

I'm on my way.

EMMA

No, wait. What is it?

FÉLICITÉ

A blind man cranking a little organ.

EMMA

Playing an air that comes from Paris.

FÉLICITÉ

That's funny. He's got in front of him a theater with a sort of room, and grotesque figures no higher than the marmousets which turn quickly. Madame would not like to come see?

EMMA

No. This same waltz is played in real rooms where women like me dance to it, abandoning themselves to their cavaliers.

(she hums for a moment)

Go, Félicité. Give him crown.

FÉLICITÉ

A crown!

EMMA

Go, I tell you, go—will you!

(Félicité leaves.)

The same waltz.

(she hums again. A second violin continues the theme.)

The same waltz.

(she gets up and starts to waltz, slowly at first—as one enthralled by an imaginary dance.)

In your arms.

(She twists about, hands hanging on emptiness, head back, eyes closed, offering her lips to an absent mouth, while the waltz loudens to an invisible orchestra.)

You, that I don't know—my beloved.

CURTAIN

ACT II
SCENE 7

The Pharmacy.

Shelves on which are aligned glass crockery with Latin labels. A counter with balancing scales. A printed blind on which a snake coils around a palm tree. A glass door on which the word "Laboratory" is scratched. It's morning. Madame Caron is chatting with Madame Homais. Both are gussied up.

MADAME CARON

Eh, my God, Madame Homais. How nice you look today.

MADAME HOMAIS

Don't speak to me about it, Madame Caron, it's Homais who insists upon it. He told me that for an event as extraordinary as the agricultural convention—and it's quite certain that water will flow in the Rieule before Yonville see them—freed me from my Spartan austerity. So, I had my cousin's marriage dress readjusted.

MADAME CARON

Serious material which ought to be kept. Silk is always good. And then, it's at once padded and suitable. I wouldn't say as much for the dress of that air-head, Madame Bovary. I just saw her crossing the market place. She's introducing a mauve skirt with five frills as big as this. And beneath this monument, no more waist than a mole-cricket.

MADAME HOMAIS

That's because she knows very well how to arrange things.

MADAME CARON

To arrange things, as you say, and also how to get things arranged.

MADAME HOMAIS

What do you mean?

MADAME CARON

It seems she bought it from Lheureux, for over a thousand. On credit, I suppose. A palatine in blue cashmere, a hanging in cotton for her room, and even a Gothic, and the Devil knows what else. As for Mr. Lheureux, he's a trickster who understands figures better than Mr. Binet. Poor Cario knows something.

MADAME HOMAIS

Perhaps we ought to put her on her guard.

MADAME CARON

Try a bit. You will see how you will be received. When folks want to end up with nothing, nothing can be done to prevent them. Think of it, Madame Homais, in a single month she spent fourteen francs for orange juice just to clean her finger nails.

MADAME HOMAIS

Not possible.

MADAME CARON

It's Polyte from the Lion d'Or, who goes with her maid who told my maid in turn.

MADAME HOMAIS

Fourteen francs to clean her nails!

MADAME CARON

Polyte talks a lot of other things, too. Imagine, once she did her hair like a man.

MADAME HOMAIS

Like a man!

MADAME CARON

Yes, Madame. Some days she dresses up like an odalisque, closes the windows in the afternoon and remains stretched on the couch with nothing to do, a book in her hand, by candlelight.

MADAME HOMAIS

Say what you will about reading, I've always had the notion that she reads too much. But, Mr. Homais conceives that she is a woman of great talents and wouldn't be out of place in a sub-prefecture.

MADAME CARON

So much the better. Only, we are not in a subprefecture. Madame Tuvache judges that she cannot receive her after the way she carried on with that young man in the Spring.

MADAME HOMAIS

You mean Mr. Léon? He left three or four months ago and has not even sent news of himself. You mustn't speak like that, Madame Caron. Doctor Bovary received him in his house and we did the same. No one finds that I am compromised, do they?

MADAME CARON

That's because in everyone's view, you are virtue itself. My late husband was accustomed—

(enter Homais, tie in hand)

HOMAIS

I was looking for you, my dear, to tie my tie. Excuse me, Madame Caron, I didn't see you and I'm in a great hurry. Yes, as for me, more confused in my laboratory than the rat in its cheese.

MADAME HOMAIS

What cheese?

HOMAIS

I wanted to convey to you that I dwell habitually like a recluse in my home. Still, today I must abandon my office because another duty calls me and I must be part of the Consultative Commission.

MADAME CARON

I didn't know you understood culture.

HOMAIS

Hey! Must one actually be an agronomist to know for oneself the labor of the earth or the fattened fowl.

MADAME HOMAIS

If you keep budging all the time. Raise your chin a bit.

HOMAIS

Please heaven that our farmers were chemists, physicians, and doctors or that at least they would listen to scientific advice.

MADAME HOMAIS

There you go again. Be nice to Madame Caron. I'm going to see if the children are ready.

HOMAIS

Fine, fine.

MADAME CARON

Until soon, Madame Homais.

(Madame Homais leaves.)

HOMAIS

And how can I serve you?

MADAME CARON

It's delicate to talk about but one cannot hide anything from you, right?

HOMAIS

Certainly. Man and the modern woman ought to show the scientist and particularly the pharmacist confidence that in less enlightened centuries they reserved for their Confessor. I am listening to you, Madame.

MADAME CARON

Here's the thing. It's nine days now that I haven't had any returns. A wash has changed nothing. I can no longer wait.

HOMAIS

Constipation, stubborn and rebellious, accompanied, no question with chronic or intermittent headaches.

MADAME CARON

I don't know.

HOMAIS

What I mean is—do you have bad headaches?

MADAME CARON

Yes—it hurts my temples.

HOMAIS

I see what it is. It shall not be said whatever the day or the time, that I allowed a patient to suffer. I am going to make two preparations which won't fail to ease you. I'll stop all other business. So much the worse for the Consultative Commission. It can wait.

MADAME CARON

Thanks.

HOMAIS

The first is meant to be absorbed by way of mouth. It isn't a question of a drastic purge but rather as a *mino vatif* whose composition is uniquely mine, and which has always given me excellent results. The second you will incorporate by a foot-bath, whose temperature will be as hot as you can stand, and whose duration will be between fifteen and twenty minutes.

MADAME CARON

I ask your pardon.

HOMAIS

Vulgo—you will pour it in a hot bath.

MADAME CARON

Ah, yes.

HOMAIS

My student will bring you these two packages in a half hour

from now, with all desired discretion.

MADAME CARON

And I'll be improved?

HOMAIS

Without delay, remission, or evasion.

MADAME CARON

Ah, I hesitated to go to the Doctor, but I'm satisfied to be put right by you.

HOMAIS

No doubt, Madame Caron, no doubt. I don't say that in particularly thorny cases the doctor ought not to be considered as more competent, thanks to experience he has had to pursue in the hospitals. But, as long as it is a case of current ills that haven't spread, it's necessary to recognize that the pharmacist, living in familiarity with remedies has a knowledge more immediate of their properties and their benefits.

(Enter Charles and Emma)

Hello, Doctor! My respects, Madame!

Come in, will you Doctor! Goodbye, Madame Caron, goodbye!

(He escorts Madame Caron out)

EMMA

We are coming to tour the fair grounds.

HOMAIS

Justin! Justin!

CHARLES

I believe you undertook to reserving places for us at the ceremony.

HOMAIS

Yours, Doctor, is, as is suitable, on the official tribunal behind Mr. Derozerays de Planville, that of Madame is beside Madame Homais, under the peristyle of the town hall. We will go there, if you like, once I have finished a work of great urgency.

(Enter Justin)

EMMA

Hello, Justin.

JUSTIN

Hello, Madame.

HOMAIS

Bring me in haste Colutea arborescens, Rhamnus cathartica, and Euphorbia lathyris. There's never a day of holiday for me. It will suffice for us to leave when the bombardment from the battery in front of the church announces the Prefect's carriage.

EMMA

What animation! Yonville is no longer recognizable.

CHARLES

It's going to be a superb day.

HOMAIS

Yes, the weather announces itself to our wishes thanks to the West Wind. Oil of croton tiglium.

EMMA

What a proud bearing Mr. Binet has in his fire-brigade uniform!

HOMAIS

Justin, the grain spatula.

CHARLES

An urgent prescription.

HOMAIS

A simple laxative for Madame Caron. I wasted my time trying to persuade her to go see you and to have a rational treatment prescribed. Always, the same routine. Justin! where is the ten gram weight?

JUSTIN

Here, sir.

HOMAIS

Put these two glasses back where they belong. Necessarily, it's an extraordinary cure which strikes the imagination with excitement. A day like today brings us proof that Progress can thrive in Yonville as well as elsewhere, despite the woeful indolence of minds. Hold on, Madame. Why, for example, doesn't your husband rid that unfortunate Hippolyte of his club foot? I've read the highest praise for a new method of operations of strephopodia. It's declared to be infallible.

CHARLES

That's not in my line.

HOMAIS

Pass me the pestle—No, the white one— Still, what risk would there be? Success almost certain, relief and improvement of the patient. Celebrity rapidly acquired by the surgeon. Hippolyte won't fail to recount his cure to all travelers. And what would prevent me from sending the newspaper a short article on the topic? An article circulates, gets talked about—it ends by snowballing. And who knows, who know?

EMMA

You ought to consider it, my friend.

CHARLES

Fine, fine. Here's Mr. Boulanger who's passing through the market.

HOMAIS

The purchaser of the Château La Hachette. Sinapsis alba. You already know him.

CHARLES

He came last week for the bleeding of a wagon driver. My wife found herself there and the next day he sent her some autumn roses.

HOMAIS

Weigh a grain meticulously, and add it into the pestle, taking care to pour it freely.

CHARLES

He's a very likable man.

HOMAIS

He himself priced his new domain. But he won't have to trouble himself because he affirmed to me that he possesses at least fifteen thousand pounds of income. Very well. Go get me the pestle of box-wood in the laboratory.

CHARLES

He's stopping to look at the pigs.

HOMAIS

I didn't want to speak before the boy. It seems he may have led the life of a rake, this Mr. Boulanger, and even now he keeps up a connection in Rouen. They even say she's an actress in a theater.

(Charles bows twice through the glass.)

CHARLES

He saw me.

(Enter Rodolphe. Large, robust, elegant. His black hair twisted in a curl over his hearty face. He wears a thick green velour coat, but his cambric shirt has folded cuffs and his boots smack of varnished leather.)

RODOLPHE

I was just going to give you a place, Doctor, for what I owe you, when I noticed you. Madame, very happy to be able to present you my respects. Mr. Homais, no doubt. I heard speak of you as a notable in the region, and congratulate myself on knowing you.

HOMAIS

Likewise, Mr. Boulanger. Be sure that if I have some enlightenment, it asks only to be employed in your service. Be so kind as to excuse the exigencies of professional duty if I do not interrupt a delicate preparation to receive you as I would desire.

RODOLPHE

Go ahead, go ahead!

CHARLES

Your driver is well set up?

RODOLPHE

Like a charm. He's over there on the fairground. I only came to supervise the folks who brought my animals.

CHARLES

But you are going to be present at the ceremony? If you don't
yet have a reserved chair on the tribunal, Mr. Homais and I are
going to employ ourselves to—

RODOLPHE

Thanks. I see it's necessary to be dressed up, and you can verify
the casualness of my dress. I wasn't expecting to meet Madame.

CHARLES

It seems to me—

RODOLPHE

And then, I confess to you I'm not eager to mix with official
characters for the joy of seeing the biggest boar, the best milk-
cow, or the prize of farm hands.

(Emma laughs)

Madame understands me.

(Cannon shot)

HOMAIS

The Prefect's carriage is signaled.

BINET'S VOICE

Take arms. Present arms!

(A fanfare covers the noise of the crowd passing before the

Pharmacy.)

HOMAIS

Justin! Finish wrapping this up and take it right away to Madame Caron.

CHARLES

Oh, the Prefect hasn't come in person.

HOMAIS

This poor Tuvache is singularly denuded of the affable dignity suitable to a mayor of the locality on such an occasion.

(The fanfares die down. Indistinct murmurs.)

CHARLES

It will be time for us to go occupy our seats.

EMMA

Decidedly, I think I like Mr. Boulanger and I prefer to avoid the mob.

HOMAIS

In that case, shall I dare to propose you remain here? You will find yourself on the side of the crowd, all resting, yet able to hear the speeches if you leave the door open a bit.

RODOLPHE

I will gladly profit by the offer if Madame authorizes me to do it.

EMMA

No question.

VOICE OF THE ORATOR

Gentlemen, allow me to be permitted first of all, and I am sure this feeling will be shared by all of you—that I may be permitted, I say—to render justice to the superior administration, and to our sovereign, to the beloved king to which no branch of the public or private prosperity is indifferent, and who governs with a firm and wise hand the chariot of state among the incessant perils of a strong sea.

(From the first words Charles is uneasy)

CHARLES

Come quickly, Mr. Homais. We will no longer be able to reach our seats without being noticed.

HOMAIS

What does it matter if we are? Everyone knows the gravity of our professions is such as to excuse a slight delay.

CHARLES

Goodbye, Mr. Boulanger. Till later, my little pussy.

(Charles and Homais leave.)

ORATOR

It's no longer time, gentlemen, in which discord embloodies your squares, when the owner, the business man, the worker himself, dozing in the evening in peace, trembles to find himself awakened by the noise of the incendiary tocsins, or where the most subversive slogans undermine audaciously—

RODOLPHE

May I close the door—?

EMMA

Why?

RODOLPHE

Do you insist on listening to snoring phrases of this village Berryer?

EMMA

No, but—

RODOLPHE (after closing the door)

And then it's better that no one notice us. With my bad reputation—

EMMA

You are slandering yourself.

RODOLPHE

Alas, no! I am sure that it is execrable, and the saddest part of it is that I deserve it. I cast myself into all sorts of adventures. I've committed a thousand follies.

EMMA

And you haven't found happiness?

RODOLPHE

Happiness wasn't there.

EMMA

Does one ever find it? At least you called it, sought it, pursued it. You haven't remained with prayerful hands, vainly hoping for it in silence, the way we poor women do.

RODOLPHE

I'd actually guessed that as soon as you appeared to me the other day. You are distracted among the mediocrities of life.

EMMA

Why do you tell me that?

RODOLPHE

Because our fates are alike.

EMMA

Come on! You haven't the experience of pain.

RODOLPHE

You imagine that because I apply the mask of a jester to my face? I've lacked so many things. If I had not a sincere affection, I would have had a goal in life. I would have nobly expended the energy of which I am capable, instead of wasting it in useless distractions. But, I am still all alone.

EMMA

A goal in life! You haven't attempted to create one for yourself, from pride, from duty?

RODOLPHE

Not that word! They are a pack of blockheads in flannel suits, and bigots in foot-warmers who sing to us continually in our ears. Eh, by Jove! Duty is to feel, to sense, what is great, to cherish what is beautiful, and not to accept all the conventions of society with the indignities they impose on us.

EMMA

Still—

RODOLPHE

Why declaim against passions? Aren't they the only good things that's certain on earth, the source of heroism, of enthusiasm, of poetry, of music, of arts, what do I know! Of everything in the end?

EMMA

It's necessary to follow a bit the opinion of the world and obey its morals.

RODOLPHE

But there are two moralities. The small one, the agreed, that which voices endlessly, brays so loud, and agitates itself lower, earth to earth. But the other, the, the great, the eternal is as far above us as the blue heaven which lights us. Is it only a sentiment that the world condemns? The most noble instincts, the purest sympathies are slandered, persecuted, and if, in the end, two poor souls meet—everything is organized so they cannot be together. But they will try, despite everything, they will beat their wings, and sooner or later they will join each other because fate exacts it, and they are born for each other.—Don't you believe that? Don't you believe it?

EMMA

I'm a little stuffy. Would you open the door?

ORATOR

And you, venerable servants, humble servants, for whom, the government until today had any consideration, the most difficult laborers, come receive the reward of your silent virtues, and be convinced that the State, henceforth, has its eyes fixed on you, that it encourages you, that it protects you, and that it will lighten as much as it is in its power the weight of your painful sacrifices.

(applause, commotion)

RODOLPHE

You were saying that you doubt happiness is ever found on earth. Sometimes, still, it appears suddenly when one is falling into despair. It's like a voice shouting, "Here it is!" The treasure that one has cherished so much, is before you, and one dares not believe it yet, so one remains dazzled as if emerging from the shadows into the light.

(Calls for silence for the proclamation of awards.)

Why do we know each other? What chance wished it? Is it through estrangement, like two flowing rivers that join—our inclinations have pushed us toward each other.

PRESIDENT

Together good cultures.

RODOLPHE

When I came to your home for the first time—

PRESIDENT

To Mr. Pizay from Quincampoix.

RODOLPHE

Could I suspect that my fate would be cast in that minute?

PRESIDENT

Seventy francs.

RODOLPHE

Perhaps, I ought to have fled, but it was already too late.

PRESIDENT

Manure.

RODOLPHE

Whatever may happen, from now on, I will remain close to you.

PRESIDENT

To Mr. Le Metell from Argueul—

RODOLPHE

This evening, tomorrow, all my life.

PRESIDENT

A gold medal—

RODOLPHE

You are the one I've always dreamed of.

PRESIDENT

To Mr. Bain, from Givry Saint Martin.

RODOLPHE

It was because of not finding you that I was consoling myself with other women.

PRESIDENT

For a Merino ram.

RODOLPHE

Don't reject me.

PRESIDENT

A bronze medal.

RODOLPHE

Be nice.

PRESIDENT

Breed of pigs.

RODOLPHE

Emma.

EMMA

Sir!

PRESIDENT.

To Mr. Collembourg, sixty francs.

RODOLPHE

Emma!

PRESIDENT

A great crab with fatty seeds.

EMMA

What do you take me for, Keep yourself for your easy conquests.
Goodbye, sir.

PRESIDENT

To Mr. Belot of Notre Dame.

RODOLPHE

I am mad.

PRESIDENT

As an incentive—ten francs.

RODOLPHE

Pardon me.

PRESIDENT

Domestic services.

EMMA

Goodbye!

(she leaves, but in the doorway, she extends her hands which he kisses.)

PRESIDENT

To Catherine-Niciase Leroux from Sassetot-La Guerrière for fifty-four years of service in the same farm.

RODOLPHE

I wanted to go too fast.

PRESIDENT

Twenty-five francs.

RODOLPHE

But she is really pretty.

(Fanfares play the air from *La Parisienne*)

CURTAIN

ACT II
SCENE 8

The Square of Yonville.

The evening of the Convention. Fleur de lys and garlands of Chinese lanterns.

Homais and Madame Lefrançois, Lheureux, and Félicité with Hipployte watch fireworks.

Emma leans on Charles's arm and Rodolphe.

FÉLICITÉ

Oh, what beautiful blue.

CHARLES

You aren't looking.

EMMA

Yes, yes.

MADAME HOMAIS

I ought to have brought the children despite the hour instead of leaving them with Justin.

FÉLICITÉ

Oh—that one.

CHARLES

It's going to fall on the side of Buchy.

(Scream by Félicité.)

MADAME LEFRANÇOIS

What's wrong with her?

FÉLICITÉ

It's the firecracker.

(To Hippolyte)

You know very well I don't like being tickled.

HIPPOLYTE

But as for me, I love tickling you.

FÉLICITÉ

Stop a bit.

CHARLES

A turning Sun.

ALL

Oh!

MADAME HOMAIS

A sheaf!

ALL

Oh!

FÉLICITÉ

Stars.

ALL

Oh!

HOMAIS

A Roman candle.

HIPPOLYTE

Cover your ears like this.

CHARLES

Look, Emma. The Church is all red.

MADAME HOMAIS

And then all green. Bravo!

(Binet enters as Captain of Firemen)

HOMAIS

Ah, Mr. Binet. I present you my congratulations for the ener-
getic authority of your commands, and the martial air of our
militia.

BINET

Pff! Pff! Conscripts. If you had seen me at Lutzen where I was
almost proposed for the Cross.

HOMAIS

Permit me to also to draw your attention to the danger of unex-
ploded squibs.

BINET

There haven't been any accidents and the firing is over.

HOMAIS

What are you saying? And the main display which is to show a
dragon gnawing its tail?

BINET

It didn't work. Your servant.

(Binet leaves)

HOMAIS

This is where the imprudence of the public powers leads. Mr.

Binet!

(Homais leaves)

HIPPOLYTE

It seems it's over.

FÉLICITÉ

Shame.

MADAME LEFRANÇOIS

It wasn't worth the trouble of making so much inconvenience.
They call this nonsense doing good for the country.

(they leave)

CHARLES

We must go home now. You must be worn out.

EMMA

No, no.

CHARLES

There's a pretty lunette that you haven't yet made.

RODOLPHE

Madame is always in delicate health.

CHARLES

Oh, nothing serious. But depression, insomnia. She must agree
to take the air, a little exercise.

RODOLPHE

Strolls on horseback. Wouldn't they be indicated?

CHARLES

Perfect. Now there's an idea. You ought to follow it.

EMMA

I don't have a mount.

RODOLPHE

Don't let that bother you. I would be happy to place one of my
horses at your disposition, and to become your squire.

EMMA

No, no, I thank you.

CHARLES

Why not accept the gracious propositions of Mr. Boulanger?

EMMA

With the small minds of the country—

RODOLPHE

Who would actually dare?

CHARLES

Ta, ta, ta. Health above all. You are wrong.

EMMA

And how would I ride a horse without a horsewoman's dress?

CHARLES

Well, you must order one.

LHEUREUX

Excuse me for meddling in your conversation. I heard without listening. I am, as always, at Madame's disposition, and can procure her a riding outfit and all that is necessary with the shortest delay.

CHARLES

Doesn't that convince you?

EMMA

Since you insist. Mr. Lheureux, come see me tomorrow morning so we can arrange all this.

(Lheureux bows and leaves)

CHARLES

Now you are being reasonable. I'm really happy, my little pussy.

RODOLPHE

You have only to give me your orders. The day that suits you I will come get you with the horses.

CHARLES

The sooner the better. I will write you, dear sir, as soon as the costume is ready. My wife will be at your disposition, and I'll trust in your complaisance to watch over her.

RODOLPHE

You can count on me.

CHARLES

A thousand thanks,

HOMAIS (returning)

Mr. Binet had given me all appeasements. No spark appears to have fallen and the pumps are full. Come on, wake up, my dear. Goodbye Monsieur and Madame. Goodbye, Mr. Boulanger. Have you merely noticed the absence of the clergy? Doubtless, the sacristans understand progress in a different way. So much the worse for the gentlemen of Loyola.

RODOLPHE

Good evening, Mr. Homais.

HOMAIS

You are right. It's time to go to sleep.

MADAME HOMAIS

My legs are going back into my body. But, never mind. We had a beautiful day.

RODOLPHE

Yes, a very fine day.

(Fanfares play the retreat.)

CURTAIN

ACT II
SCENE IX

Little by little the fanfares give way to the orchestra and the retreat melds into a waltz. The same waltz we heard on the organ-grinder; the violin separates from the theme and the stage lights up: the Beauties appear.

BEAUTIES

Again one is caught in a trap.
The grain of wheat flows under the millstone.
All he had to do was come and say the words she was waiting
    for.
He's a lad who knows women.
He knows the words that need to be said.
Always the same, right?
Always the same.
But she wept for hearing them only in a dream.
She had shivered from fear of dying without hearing them.
The gallop of horses.
The road under the branches.
The silence in the heart of the forest.
The silence and weariness of Autumn.
Flowery, noisy
Golden trees,
Bitter perfumes.
The rustling of dead leaves.

(The bedroom of Madame Bovary lights up. Under white curtains Emma is sleeping beside Charles, who is dozing wearing a blue silk kerchief on his head.)

EMMA

I have a lover!

BEAUTIES

Magnificent name, swollen with pride, heavy with caresses.

EMMA

I have a lover.

A BEAUTY

Haloed with an aura of sin.

EMMA

To say that returning I found on the road the tracks of our horses, as if nothing had changed!

BEAUTIES

What—the same wave is coming to beat the sonorous shore.
What, at the depth of the valley, the same clocks are greeting
    such a dawn as this?
The same wind, twisted, shaking the moaning black pines?
The boat-men along the length of the stream, rhythmically
    stamp their feet to the same song?

EMMA

I'm a new person. A new blood is circulating in my flesh like a stream of milk.

BEAUTIES

No. You are yourself. You've found yourself. That's the call one
    cannot resist.
The breath from which there is no shelter.
Rise up, therefor, desired storms.

EMMA

He's handsome.

BEAUTIES

He was handsome.
They were all handsome. But who cares!
Who cares who one loves? The divine thing is to love.

EMMA

Joy! The fever of joy!

BEAUTIES

Nothing will count again after the joy of giving oneself, despite
    duty, and despite God.
With all your heart? With all your body?

EMMA

I have a lover!

BEAUTIES

The intoxication of distraction. The ecstasy of abandonment.
Annihilation.

EMMA

I have love.

(Charles snores. Night absorbs the room.)

THE BEAUTIES

Poor little girl.
We, too, thought to be happy.
A year.
A month.
A week.
One night.
But when you remember your life, is it not this night that
    counts?

(They disappear in their turn. A hunting horn in the distance.)

CURTAIN

ACT II

SCENE 10

Rodolphe's room.

Winter at dawn. Braziers blaze in the large chimney surmounted by a large stag. Rodolphe enters a cloak thrown over his house robe.

RODOLPHE (to his valet)

Run now to Neufchatel with the carriage and bring back the Vet. Until he arrives don't let the calf suckle. For Noiraude, have Marette give him a slice of toast in warm wine. That will set him up. If she still pulls her tongue, some water, but tepid and diluting with coarse flour.

GÉRARD

Yes, master. I'm on my way.

RODOLPHE

Gérard. With all this cold and snow, make sure not to leave open the stable door. Put him in the care of Vasselot and the kid. I'm going back to bed and sleep—not too soon. But when the Vet arrives, you'll come wake me up.

GÉRARD

Yes, master. (he leaves)

RODOLPHE

It's freezing here.

(he tosses some firewood into the fire, and turns at a noise at the door. Emma is in the doorway.)

You! You! At this hour!

EMMA

I love you.

RODOLPHE

How were you able to come?

EMMA

My husband was called before dawn. A birth.

RODOLPHE

This is the day.

EMMA

You say.

RODOLPHE

Nothing. I'm contemplating you.

EMMA

I had need—need to see you right away. I dressed running and I came by the shore. Heaven was just beginning to go pale. From the distance I saw your weather vane cut up, and I repeated to myself, "It's the house of my lover." I ran. A moment went by and I became uneasy. "How will I get in? Everything will be locked." But no. Everything was open. Miraculously, as if the walls rolled up by themselves at my approach.

RODOLPHE

Your dress is wet.

EMMA

That's because it snowed last night. My feet were the first to burrow through the snow.

RODOLPHE

Come near the fire. Give me your feet and I will warm them.

EMMA

Here.

RODOLPHE

Naked.

EMMA

Here. But how come you are up so early?

RODOLPHE

I was thinking too much about you to be able to sleep.

EMMA

You really love me so much?

RODOLPHE

Don't you know it?

EMMA

Wait! Wait! I'm made like a gypsy. A pipe. I didn't know that you smoked a pipe. Let me see.

RODOLPHE

Pff! Pff!

EMMA

My turn now! Pfff! Pff!

RODOLPHE

It's nice to see you a little gay. I was afraid you wouldn't succeed in ridding yourself of your sadness.

EMMA

The other day you told me the same thing about my modesty. Are you reassured, my handsome Rodolphe?

RODOLPHE

Are you going to renounce your melancholy airs once and for all?

EMMA

Give me time. I'm not used to being happy. I need to accustom myself to it, little by little. You know the noise the wind makes in the winter in abandoned houses. The engulfing pain was in me with the same sweet howling, and I was cold in my soul. It was the right time for you to come.

RODOLPHE

What's the good of rehashing the past. What was, and what is no more.

EMMA

You are right. I no longer want to think about anything except the future.

RODOLPHE

The present, first of all.

EMMA

It's the same thing. Aren't you my present and my future? Listen. I've discovered a fissure in the wall of my terrace. Every morning I'll put a letter in it. You'll come get it and you must leave another in its place.

RODOLPHE

Every day?

EMMA

Yes, every day. A long letter. It's sworn?

RODOLPHE

If you wish.

EMMA

Swear to me, also, that every night at midnight you will think of your mistress.

RODOLPHE

I swear it.

EMMA

I've brought you your reward. You've confessed to me, that often, in the evening, you came to Yonville, and stayed in the path by the shore to watch the light from my windows over the gate. Poor friend.

RODOLPHE

Me, I told you that?

EMMA

A long while ago. I didn't forget it. Here's the key to the gate. Keep it. I will tell Charles it is lost. At night, when you wish,

you can enter. We will agree on a signal. I will fly to meet you—
in winter in the consulting room, in summer beneath the arbor.

RODOLPHE

How sweet you are!

EMMA

No, but such as I am, I am yours. We will take our place in the
parade of great lovers. We shall be like Laura and Petrarch.

RODOLPHE (ironic)

Dante and Beatrice.

EMMA

Héloïse and Abelard.

RODOLPHE

You don't prefer another example?

EMMA

I am sure that on high, God blesses our union. Tell me you've
never loved other women. Don't laugh.

RODOLPHE

Do you imagine you've taken me as a virgin?

EMMA

None has held the place in your heart that you've given me?

RODOLPHE

You know that very well. Why do you want me to repeat it?

EMMA

What were their names?

RODOLPHE

What do their names matter?

EMMA

Show me their pictures.

RODOLPHE

Where are they? Have I even kept them?

EMMA

Why indeed, you have souvenirs, relics, letters shut up in some precious box?

RODOLPHE

A precious box? Look in the secretary—a box of biscuits from Reims.

EMMA

Can I open it?

RODOLPHE

If you like. It ought to have some things of the sort you're talking about.

EMMA

It smells of withered roses. A black mask.

RODOLPHE

Carlotta.

EMMA

A garter. A bouquet. Some blonde hairs. Who was that?

RODOLPHE

Ursula. A little modiste, or Anaïs, a dancer, or Sophia.

EMMA

A ribbon, Another garter. Always blonde hairs. These are really fine. And ashes—of what?

RODOLPHE

I don't know any more.

EMMA

A yellow glove. She had a large hand. Black hair. Like the wing of a crow.

RODOLPHE

Hortense.

EMMA

A kerchief. A white glove.

RODOLPHE

What a bunch of jokes.

EMMA

Some carrot-red hair.

RODOLPHE

She was the first. My sister's tutor. I was sixteen, she was forty. Extremes sleep together as the other one said.

EMMA

Carrot-red hair. Rodolphe, I want to burn all this.

RODOLPHE

Burn it, go ahead.

(They watch the flames in silence.)

EMMA

Thanks. Now there's only me.

RODOLPHE

Child!

EMMA

I can be myself alone. All those others. Some may have been more beautiful, but none knew how to love like me. I will be whatever you like. You have freed me from myself. My happiness is no longer belonging to myself. I belong to you, and am no more than a great flame burning for you, to be used, at your pleasure, and to lose myself in you.

RODOLPHE

My cherished child. Come.

THE BEAUTIES (returning as the forestage is lit up)

He will take me away on the crup of his horse and we will gallop
    toward the sea shore.
He will hide me in his cloak and my cheek will get bruised
    against the embroidery of his vest, and at the place I listen,
    his heart will beat my name.
My life has the smell of his hair.
My life has the taste of his mouth.
I saw my joy in the depth of his eyes.

CURTAIN

ACT II
SCENE 11

The pharmacy.

Homais is trying hard to persuade Hipployte.

HOMAIS

I don't understand such blindness—to refuse the benefits of science. A simple sting, like a little bloodletting, less than the removal of a corn. What do you say?

HIPPOLYTE

We'll see.

HOMAIS

Picture yourself how you will feel, more strapping and more alert. What do you say?

HIPPOLYTE

We'll see.

HOMAIS

Aren't you a man, by jiminy? Aren't you ashamed to be afraid? What would happen, really, if you'd had to serve, to fight under the flag?

HIPPOLYTE

Till next time, Mr. Homais.

HOMAIS

Think that this won't cost you anything.

HIPPOLYTE

Nothing at all?

HOMAIS

Absolutely nothing. Doctor Bovary will actually furnish the machine for the operation. What do you say to that?

HIPPOLYTE

We'll see.

(He leaves. Madame Homais appears.)

MADAME HOMAIS

Mr. Homais.

HOMAIS

What lack of enlightenment in this clubfoot.

MADAME HOMAIS

Mr. Homais.

HOMAIS

What, my sweet?

MADAME HOMAIS

I'm bringing you a book.

HOMAIS

You—a book!

MADAME HOMAIS

It fell from Justin's pocket as he was bending over to pick up a basin of jam. It disgusts me, but I let you judge.

HOMAIS

Give me. Conjugal love. Ah, very nice, very nice, very nice. And engravings.

MADAME HOMAIS

Take a look.

HOMAIS

Move away. Don't soil your eyes. Ah, this is too much! Go bring me the guilty one!

(Madame Homais leaves. Homais strides back and forth, Justin enters.)

Until when—wretched child, will you abuse our patience? So this is how you reward me for the paternal cares I've lavished on you? Where would you be without me? Who furnished you with food, education, clothing, all the means of appearing with honor in the ranks of society? I'm beginning to terribly repent of having taken charge of your person. You live like a cock in pie to stuff yourself. You have no aptitude for science. You barely know how to paste on a label. And that's not all, you reach the point of introducing into my house an infamous publication. Why, so you have actually all the vices, little wretch! Didn't you consider that this book could fall into the hands of my children, corrupt Napoléon, tarnish the purity of Athalia? I open at random.

(a pause as he reads)

It's not that I disapprove entirely of the work. The author is a doctor; there are certain aspects of science that it is not bad for a man to know. I dare say that it is important for a man to know. But not at your age.

JUSTIN

I'm seventeen.

HOMAIS

Don't think me the slave of reactionary prejudices when I shall judge that that the hour for initiation has struck, I shall not hesitate to lead you myself to Rouen, to the Temple of Cythera that I used to frequent myself, and which, from the point of view of hygiene, will present all the desired guarantees. But from now, till then, don't run the risk of perverting your imagination by reading things like this.

(he reads, a pause.)

All things considered, weighing the pros and the cons, the practical conclusion of this incident may well be that I will accompany to you to Rouen, as soon as next week.

JUSTIN

I don't want that.

HOMAIS

What are you saying?

JUSTIN

I don't want that.

HOMAIS

You refuse to discover the secrets of Nature! Do you really intend to make a monk of yourself? Or rather, would you be so precociously taken by a skirt that your only thought is to raise another?

JUSTIN

That's not true.

HOMAIS

I've smelled it from a distance for a long time. I understand why you so assiduously frequent the house of Madame Bovary.

JUSTIN

You don't have the right—

HOMAIS

Dare deny that you were increasing your intrigues, Faublas!

JUSTIN

I don't allow you—

HOMAIS

Dare to deny that you are courting the maid!

JUSTIN

The maid!

HOMAIS

Dare deny it! Lovelace!

MADAME HOMAIS (running in at the shouting)

Lord, my God! What's going on?

JUSTIN

It's nothing!

HOMAIS

Imagine—he doesn't want me to take him—That's fine. Get out. Leave me in peace.

(They leave. Homais sits down to read.)

CURTAIN

ACT II

SCENE 12

The garden of Bovary's house.

Moonlight. A bench under a Wisteria tree.

EMMA (calling low)

Rodolphe! Rodolphe!

RODOLPHE

Here!

EMMA

I thought he would never end gossiping before going to bed. I was going crazy thinking you were so near, so near, and that he was making me wait, making me seem to read, not to run and throw myself in your arms. Open your cloak. Clasp me to you. Envelop me completely.

RODOLPHE

How large your eyes appear and how they shine in the night.

EMMA

Hug me tighter, my lover. I've got only you in the world.

RODOLPHE

What's wrong, poor angel? You are trembling with fever.

EMMA

What's wrong? You recall the dirty tricks of the apothecary, for the club foot at the Lion d'or—to get him to let Charles operate on him?

RODOLPHE

Well?

EMMA

It's over with, their operation. Three days ago. The result is that today he had to go to Rouen in all haste to find a surgeon, to amputate Hippolyte's leg. I heard him scream in my room.

RODOLPHE

Gangrene set in?

EMMA

I don't know. I don't want to know. Charles made a mistake, Afterwards, during the evenings, he'd hide his head in his hands; he read and re-read his book! The Doctor from Rouen humiliated him before the whole world by reproaching him for his ignorance and clumsiness.

RODOLPHE

The poor lad.

EMMA

It's him that you pity! He dared to come to tell me this so I could console him. I'm ashamed, Rodolphe. I'm choked with shame.

RODOLPHE

Calm down.

EMMA

I'm weary enough of my life beside this mediocrity. The poor lad, you say! Yes, the poor lad.

RODOLPHE

A little patience.

EMMA

I've been patient for years. Each evening I await his return with more disgust than in the morning, and I don't know how to prevent myself from spying on his gestures, always the same. I've had enough of it. I no longer want to see him.

RODOLPHE

You are exaggerating.

EMMA

Why did I marry him? A man—ought he not to know everything, to initiate you to the energies of the passions, to the refinements of life, to all the mysteries? This one teaches nothing, knows nothing, wants nothing. His conversation is flat, like a sidewalk. And the worst is that he expands, serenely well seated in life. I hate him for the happiness I give him, for that he thinks to give me. Rodolphe, I can't take it anymore. Save me!

RODOLPHE

Is there something I can do?

EMMA

You have only to want to.

RODOLPHE

What must be done? What do you want?

EMMA

Take me away! Carry me off!

RODOLPHE

You Are mad!

EMMA

I beg you. We will go live somewhere else, truly live.

RODOLPHE

If you consider the obstacles—

EMMA

You hesitate. I'm offering you my whole life.

RODOLPHE

Listen to the language of reason.

EMMA

Reason, duty, opinion. What else? Would I be yours if I listened to them?

RODOLPHE

Still—

EMMA

Shut up! It's necessary to choose if you want me. Come to my aide, take me away from here. If not, if it's too much to ask of you, let's separate, let's finish immediately.

RODOLPHE

You are not speaking seriously?

EMMA

Choose!

RODOLPHE

Understand, will you—

EMMA

Yes, or no?

RODOLPHE

Give me time—

EMMA

Ah, you no longer love me!

RODOLPHE

Why, yes. Only I cannot uproot my affairs in a minute. My engagements, the routine of my life. There are measures to take, a thousand things to settle. And you yourself—

EMMA

As for me, I have nothing in the world. You are everything for me. And yourself—

RODOLPHE

I want you more every day.

EMMA

Truly?

RODOLPHE

Yes.

EMMA

Then you are good with me? Take the time you need to make your preparations. A month, six weeks. Look, until July.

RODOLPHE

That's about right. Until July.

EMMA

And tell me that in July everything will be over!

RODOLPHE

It will be over, since you wish it.

EMMA

Ah, Rodolphe! Rodolphe! It seems to me that at the moment that I'm shaking in the Mail Coach; it will be as if we were flying towards the clouds! Four galloping horses will carry us toward the country from which we will never return.

RODOLPHE

Consider—

EMMA

Imagine. We will climb escarped routes listening to the song of the postilion, who will repeat it in the mountain echo. From the top of a hill we will discover some splendid city, with domes, ships, orange forests and cathedrals of white marble. We will hear the sound of clocks, the vibrations of guitars, the murmur of fountains.

RODOLPHE

My poor little girl.

EMMA

And then one evening we will arrive in a village of fishermen where brown nets are drying in the wind, the length of the cliff. There it will be good to be. Our house will be low—with a flat roof, under a palm tree by the sea.

RODOLPHE

Emma!

EMMA

The days will be like the hammock in which we will swing. And the nights, my love, the sweet nights, starry and warm—

RODOLPHE

Emma darling.

EMMA

Why are you so sad?

RODOLPHE

I am not sad.

EMMA

Yes, I understand. It's because of all that you must break off.

RODOLPHE

Yes, of all that I'm going to have to break off.

EMMA

You have until July. Almost two months more.

RODOLPHE

Two months.

EMMA

You must love me.

RODOLPHE

I've never loved you as much as this evening. I didn't know you loved me so much.

EMMA

My handsome Rodolphe.

RODOLPHE

Visualize everything carefully. There's still time. Perhaps you will repent.

EMMA

Never! There's no desert that I won't cross with you. As we live together it will be like a clasp. Each day more close together, more complete. We will be alone with each other eternally.

(The Curtain falls slowly. A violin plays the tune of the waltz.)

C U R T A I N

ACT II

SCENE 13

Rodolphe's room at La Hachette.

Rodolphe's room slowly appears. A sunny afternoon of golden July slits through closed shutters.

RODOLPHE

She was a pretty mistress. More charming still, in these last two months. But, all the same it would have been too stupid to expatriate myself. These difficulties, these expenses. How she shone just now saying, "It's for tomorrow. The road to Genes. We will have good weather. It will be good to travel." Poor kid. Say, will you, my lad, you're growing old. There you are, sentimental. Come on.

(he sits at his desk and starts to write.)

"Courage, Emma, courage. You won't find me in Rouen. I don't want to do harm to your life." The strangest part is that it's true. I am acting in her interest. "Do you know the abyss I was dragging you into, poor angel? Alas, why were you so beautiful?"

(as he continues to write, his room disappears and Emma's room appears. The room is in great disorder, armoires open, drawers wide open. Emma comes and goes, slightly impatient, overflowing with happiness.)

EMMA

Félicité.

FÉLICITÉ

Here I am.

(A pause. Félicité enters.)

EMMA

Here. Take this dress for yourself.

FÉLICITÉ

Oh, thank you, Madame.

EMMA

You can also keep the two hanging under the shelf in the cabinet. Are you satisfied?

FÉLICITÉ

For sure, Madame.

EMMA

You will be beautiful to please your friend with it.

FÉLICITÉ

But, I—

EMMA

No use lying. I know everything. It's the notary's servant.

FÉLICITÉ

You must believe—

EMMA

Don't blush, will you, little idiot. Do I seem to be reproaching you? You are right, if you love him.—Have you finished the ironing?

FÉLICITÉ

Not yet, Madame. It's not for me to complain, but this time I have three baskets. You would say it's the trousseau of a newlywed.

EMMA

Hurry up. It needs to be ready this evening.

FÉLICITÉ

I will try.

(The bell rings. Félicité looks outside.)

FÉLICITÉ

It's that Lheureux again. You never see anything but his face around here anymore.

EMMA

Keep your reflections to yourself and show him in.

(Félicité leaves, Emma shuts the drawers.)

Well, have you got everything?

LHEUREUX

Have I ever failed in my word, Madame? You told me you needed it today without fail. Everything is at my place as agreed.

EMMA

The trunk?

LHEUREUX

The model of Lavasalle's shop. Bulging wide, hung with pig skin.

EMMA

And the night bag?

LHEUREUX

In tapestry, doubly lined with strong cloth, a clasp of hog wood.

EMMA

And the cloak?

LHEUREUX

As you indicated in the fitting. The worker has added a second collar, and a body in extra light tartan.

EMMA

Thanks, Mr. Lheureux. Tomorrow at five I shall leave on the Hirondelle. I'm going to Rouen/ Would you be so agreeable as to come take the suitcase in the same manner, and take it to the carriage even if it be in broad daylight?

LHEUREUX

That's the least of things.

EMMA

The cloak and the night bag. I will find them at your place. I will spend a final moment there. When you arrive during the night have Félicité tell me you are in the garden. Then till then, and thanks again.

LHEUREUX

Madame will excuse me, I still have a word to say to her, I still have a word to say to her. I allowed myself to bring my bill.

EMMA

Give it to me.

LHEUREUX

Believe me, I really regret to be obliged to do it, and I wanted to wait still, but a merchant is not his own master.

EMMA

It's quite natural. Give it to me.

LHEUREUX

May Madame take the trouble to read it.

EMMA

Ho ho!

LHEUREUX

Hell, we have here two years of various furnishings. May Madame verify it. Most of the articles were exceptionally advantageous, but as a result of adding one on top of the other—an addition is an addition, right? See, the prayer-stool, the riding habit, the cashmere, the saddle with a silver pummel, the leg of wood improved with a joint spring, a woolen rug—

EMMA

Yes, yes,—I'm not arguing.

LHEUREUX

The trunk, the night bag, the cloak do not appear on this list. I made a little note aside, that is here.

EMMA

Very well. I will settle with you for all that.

LHEUREUX

It's that unfortunately, I must insist on being paid this very day.

EMMA

What do you mean today?

LHEUREUX

Alas, I'm forced to do so.

EMMA

I wouldn't know how to suddenly dispose of a sum as large as that.

LHEUREUX

Consider that I find myself pursued and that all my capital is absent.

EMMA

It's impossible.

LHEUREUX

I cannot wait any longer.

EMMA

Since I don't have the money!

LHEUREUX

You will tell me that at least I may keep these latest furnishings. I mean the articles of travel that are still in my home.

EMMA

Don't do that!

LHEUREUX

Or I could speak to Dr. Bovary—if he settles with me tonight, this last bill, perhaps we'll find some accommodation for the other.

EMMA

No.

LHEUREUX

No?

EMMA

It's not necessary.

LHEUREUX

Then what do you want to become of me?

(Emma tosses her necklace and her watch on the table.)

EMMA

Here. Pay yourself out of these.

LHEUREUX

Oh, Madame Bovary, I am sure that you want this jewel. The watch is beautiful, the necklace is heavy. Still, one sells ill when time is urgent. I would be far from finding the amount due me.

(She tears off her wedding ring.)

EMMA

And with this?

LHEUREUX

Your wedding ring! You aren't thinking of it. You mustn't separate from it. That brings bad luck.

EMMA

Bah. He'll give me another ring.

LHEUREUX

Listen, Madame Bovary. We are going to agree some other way. I don't want the troubles that are overwhelming me to reach you by ricochet. Take back your watch and your ring.

EMMA

What have you to propose to me?

LHEUREUX

Let's suppose the bill paid; let's speak no more of it. It's as if I myself had given you the equivalent sum. You follow me?

EMMA

Yes—well?

LHEUREUX

You are going to sign a little bill of exchange for me—payable in three months, on which my friend Vincart, who's a banker in Rouen will advance me what he can. I know your signature is worth something because your husband has delegated a general power to you. A man of science cannot embarrass himself with the practical details of his life. Do this and both of us will be out of difficulties.

EMMA

If you wish. But hurry, hurry!

LHEUREUX

I expected in advance that there would have to be some other expedient, and I had in all chance prepared the note. Read it. Naturally, I was obliged to figure in Vincart's commission, and the interest he won't fail to insist on, as is perfectly just.

EMMA (signing)

Agreed! Agreed! There you go!

LHEUREUX

It's better, believe me. And if it suits you, nothing will prevent you at the end of three months—nothing—will prevent you carrying forward or extending the date a little later, or signing another note.

EMMA

You will be reimbursed before that. I will send you this money. Yes, I will have it brought to you.

LHEUREUX

No rush. Don't torture yourself over such a small thing. And accept my excuses again. Necessity makes the law.

EMMA

Yes, doesn't it. Till later, Mr. Lheureux.

(He leaves. Emma beats these worries off with a gesture and reopens the drawers, humming. La Hachette lights up again. Both rooms are now visible simultaneously.)

RODOLPHE (rereading his letter)

"I will be far away when you read these sad lines. I wanted to flee all the more quickly to avoid the temptation of seeing you again. Adieu! Keep the memory of the wretch that ruined you. Goodbye again." No. briefly. "God be with you." It almost needs tears over it.

(he pours water into a cup, soaks his fingers in it and lets a drop fall.)

My poor Emma. I really loved her.

(he seals the letter. Emma is still humming happily.)

Gérard!

GÉRARD

Sir!

EMMA

Félicité.

FÉLICITÉ (off)

Here I am.

RODOLPHE

Bring up the basket of apricots that Vasselot packed.

(Félicité enters Emma's room. Gérard brings the basket. Rodolphe hides the letter in the basket, and covers it with fruits.)

EMMA

Lheureux will soon bring a large trunk. You'll inform me without the Doctor noticing.

FÉLICITÉ

Understood.

EMMA

It's necessary to put the linen you've folded in it, and also that which is carefully chosen in the cabinet. You will go down to the woodpile with what I've finished preparing here.

FÉLICITÉ

To the woodpile.

EMMA

Yes, the trunk will remain tonight in the woodpile, and I will take it tomorrow to Rouen. There are objects I expect to exchange for others that will please me more. I don't want my husband to suspect anything until the thing is done.

FÉLICITÉ

Fine, Madame.

EMMA

Help me to arrange this.

RODOLPHE

You are going to carry this right away to Madame Bovary. Delicately. Don't deliver it to anyone except herself, to her own hands.

GÉRARD

Fine, master.

RODOLPHE

If she asks you for news of me, you will only reply that I am going to leave on a trip. You've understood.

GÉRARD

Yes, master.

RODOLPHE

Go—and be careful.

(Gérard leaves)

Oof!

EMMA

If tomorrow evening I don't come back with the Hirondelle, don't be very surprised. It might be that I am detained by this business. Hivert will bring a letter from me for my husband.

FÉLICITÉ

I will take good care of the Doctor while Madame isn't here.

EMMA

Yes. Take good care of him.

FÉLICITÉ

Shall I finish folding things?

EMMA

Go.

(Félicité leaves.)

(Rodolphe has taken the miniature of Emma, a package of letters, a ribbon, a glove, a kerchief, some dried flowers.

(Emma keeps opening boxes and taking out objects. She finds her bridal crown, tries it on, smiling, shrugs her shoulders and rejects it.

(Shrugging his shoulders, Rodolphe finds the old biscuit box and puts in his souvenir of Emma then closes the box.

(Emma collapses in a chaise-longue, eyes closed, exhausted.

(Rodolphe stuffs himself into his arm chair, lights a pipe. The light in Rodolphe's room goes out.)

FÉLICITÉ (calling from downstairs)

Madame, here's Gérard from La Hachette bringing you something.

(Emma goes to the door and leans out.)

EMMA

Gérard, Come up, will you, my friend.

GÉRARD (placing the basket)

Here's what our master sends you.

EMMA

Beautiful apricots. How nice they smell.

GÉRARD

He ordered me to give it to you in your own hands.

EMMA

Ah? And how is your master?

GÉRARD

He's getting ready to go on a trip.

EMMA

Yes, yes, I know. Goodbye.—Félicité, offer him a cup of cider.

(Gérard leaves. She smiles.)

He's getting ready to go on a trip.

(she overturns the basket. The apricots roll out and reveal the letter.)

I was sure of it, my adored Rodolphe. You weren't capable of remaining the whole day without writing me.

(She kisses the letter and continues humming the air from the waltz.)

He's preparing to go on a trip.

(She unfolds the letter and begins to read. She stops. Goes pale., resumes reading, staggers, tries again to read, and, without a sound falls into a faint.)

CURTAIN

ACT III
SCENE 14

A lodge in the balcony of the Rouen theater. Tarnished gold and dusty red velour.

Emma and Charles are seated against the light. The first act of Lucia di Lammermoor *is nearly over. One notices, yellowed by the stage, the enchanted foliage of a romantic forest. The singers' voices can be heard. The curtain lowers slowly. Applause explodes.*

PUBLIC

Bravo! Bravo! Bravo, Legardy!

EMMA

Bravo! Bravo!

CHARLES

Be careful! You are going to tear your gloves.

EMMA

Who cares! Isn't this magnificent?

CHARLES

Yes, I'm beginning to be amused. Only, I don't understand very well. Why did the gentleman in the chocolate velour—is he going to persecute her?

EMMA

Him! He's her lover.

CHARLES

Still, he swore to avenge himself on her family, and the other fellow, the little blonde with a green cloak, said, a moment before, "I love Lucia, and I think I am loved." And then he left with his father, arm in arm.

EMMA

His father?

CHARLES

The fat bearded one who wears a cock's feather in his hat. He's really the father of the young girl?

EMMA

Not at all.

CHARLES

Because I like to figure things out and the music is annoying. It blots out many words.

(Knocking on the door of the lodge. Charles opens it. It's Léon.)

Mr. Léon, what a surprise!

LÉON

I noticed you from below, and rushed to present my civilities to you.

EMMA

Then you are actually in Rouen?

LÉON

Foe a few weeks. I have to spend two years here in deep study before breaking off my Norman affairs. They are totally different from those one leads in Paris.

(Noise from the audience that mills around during the intermission.)

MERCHANTS

Oranges. Mentholated lozenges!

CHARLES

You have profited famously from the Latin Quarter. What a fine appearance! It makes it a pleasure to see you. Before you were a bit pale.

LÉON

Doubtless the heat at the bar.

CHARLES

You've grown stronger and gained confidence. It's noticeable from the first look.

MERCHANTS

Cheminots. Real cheminots.

LÉON

I didn't think, coming to the theater this evening, of having the pleasure of seeing you again. You are actually situated to come here sometimes?

EMMA

Never. It took a doctor's order.

CHARLES

Because my wife has given us a great deal of worry. She's been ill.

LÉON

And I knew nothing about it.

CHARLES

One evening last July, returning home from my rounds, I found her on the floor like a wax statue. Mr. Homais thinks that the odor from a basket of apricots would have sufficed to provoke this syncope. As for me, I don't know what to believe. Anything is possible with her—she's a true sensitive.

EMMA

You are boring Mr. Léon with this story.

LÉON

For goodness sakes! Tell me, Doctor, tell me.

CHARLES

Next morning, cerebral fever declared itself. Forty-three days, my fine friend, I spent forty-three days at her bedside, fighting death for her. And she didn't get up until November, and dragged still all winter.

EMMA

Skip all that. It's not interesting.

CHARLES

At the announcement at this gala of the famous Lagardy, I concluded nothing would be more profitable. You need distractions during convalescence. So we decided to come despite the weariness, the upset, and we must really say, the expense. I don't regret it, since she seems happy.

EMMA

Isn't this Lagardy fabulous?

LÉON

He's far from as good as Persiana and Grisi that I applauded in this same role, but still he remains excellent.

CHARLES

He alone made more noise than the entire orchestra.

LÉON

Did you know that he was a caulker in Biarritz? A Polish Princess became amorous one night as he was singing on the beach refitting some sloops. She ruined herself because of him. Now they say he's engaged in England with a heap of appointments. He travels with his cook and his three mistresses.

CHARLES

Three!

EMMA

They must have a beautiful life. To commune in the adoration of a great being, to share his weariness and his pride, to gather the flowers that people throw him, to knit his cloths.

MERCHANTS

Oranges. Menthol wafers.

CHARLES

You see that my wife is still the same. Where does she get all her ideas from! But now that you are in our country, I hope that you will come to Yonville from time to time.

LÉON

Surely, if I'm certain that I won't be importunate. How are the Homais?

CHARLES

They prosper. The children are shooting up. Franklin had a jaundice.

LÉON

And Mr. Binet?

CHARLES

He's still twisting his napkin. His house ought to be full of them.

LÉON

And Madame Lefrançois? And Polyte?

CHARLES

On that side we had a mistake.

(Emma starts fanning herself and lets out a loud sigh.)

What's wrong with you?

EMMA

A little vertigo.

CHARLES

The smell of gas—also, perhaps the need to take something. I was so afraid of missing the beginning that we presented ourselves before the doors of the theater which was still closed, without having swallowed a bouillon. I am going to go see what they might have for you in the tap room.

LÉON

Allow me.

CHARLES

No, no. Stay put. I know what she needs.

(Charles leaves)

MERCHANTS

The life of the celebrated Lagardy with his lithographed portrait.

LÉON

Do you feel better?

EMMA

It was nothing this time. But why did God not take me? Why did he leave me a useless life? You have ripened during this time, in the excitement of the great city.

LÉON

Don't believe that. If I've truly ripened, it's because a thought was dwelling in me, raising me above myself.

EMMA

Ah, truly.

(Ringing for the Second Act.)

What's that?

LÉON

Soon it will be the end of the intermission.

EMMA

Already! Well, what were you starting to tell me?

LÉON

I don't know if I dare.

EMMA

You were telling me what you thought of Paris.

LÉON

Often I went the length of the streets so as to avoid the noise of the crowd, without being able to banish the obsession which pursued me. On the boulevard at a print merchant, an Italian engraving represented a muse, I remained for hours entirely. She resembled you a little. Sometimes I imagined that some chance was bringing you, and I ran after all the carriages from whose window a veil like yours floated.

EMMA

Why?

LÉON

Why?

EMMA

Yes.

LÉON

Because I have always loved you.

(a pause)

EMMA

I didn't interrupt you.

LÉON

I had only to close my eyes to see the furniture of your house, the cradle of wisteria, your blue dress with the frills, a collar in which your chin was tucked a bit, sweetly, when you lowered your head.

EMMA

I'm listening.

LÉON

I lived for the memory of our strolls, our readings, our tête-à-têtes by the corner of the fire, our poor Sunday soirées with the pharmacist. When, in the Summer mornings the Sun rapped on the blinds, each window became for me, yours, and it was your two naked arms which passed between the flowers.

EMMA

Keep talking.

LÉON

I was very timid and you must have found me ridiculous. One time, for example,—but no question—you don't remember.

EMMA

Keep talking.

LÉON

I came to your home at the moment you were ready to leave. You had a hat with small mauve flowers. Without invitation from you, I accompanied you despite myself. At each moment, I was more and more aware of my stupidity, and yet I continued to walk beside you, not daring to outright follow you, and not wanting to leave you.

(The three raps. The stage rises. The orchestra attacks the overture of the second act. Charles returns carrying a cup.)

CHARLES

I had great trouble getting through. And, my word, I thought I was stuck there! Drink that, my little pussy.

VOICES IN THE AUDIENCE

Hush!

CHARLES

In the crunch, I unfortunately poured half over the shoulders of a lady.

VOICES

Hush!

EMMA

Shut up, will you!

CHARLES

But since the curtain hasn't risen?

VOICES

Out the door!

(The curtain rises on a gothic room and the opera continues)

CURTAIN

ACT III
SCENE 15

A room in the Hotel of the Emperors in Rouen.

A large low door with a raised sill; a bolt of heavy iron makes a white stain amidst red damask. Curtains over a large bed in the form of a sea shell that descend to the floor. In an angle a paper screen depicts persons violently colored. Golden reflections shine from curtain hooks at the top of the bed to the nails on the furniture. But everything is old-fashioned and withered.

EMMA

Every Tuesday, my love, every Tuesday will be ours now. I told my husband that I must either give up the piano at last or come take lessons every week in Rouen. I was sure of his reply. You remember. He's quite proud of me, the poor man, since all my fingers run on the keys.

LÉON

The way you know how to lie.

EMMA

It is quite necessary.

LÉON

You are a demon.

EMMA

Tell me, will you give me good lessons, my darling?

LÉON

You are an angel.

EMMA

Soon you will take me to dine in the islands. I want to feel your arm around my waist in the depth of the boat, and taste the salt sea wind on your face in the shade of poplars.

LÉON

I want what you want.

EMMA

What have you done since our last kisses? You have a bad look. I am sure you are working too much. Or what do you let your comrades drag you to? Don't see them. Don't do anything but think of us.

LÉON

I do nothing else. My boss has even scolded me.

EMMA

Bah—forget it.

LÉON

But you, what have you become? Your eyes are actually larger.

EMMA

You know very well what my life in Yonville is.

LÉON

No. I know what the life of a woman that you resemble was, and that I left there. But the one I've found is quite different, and I know nothing of it.

EMMA

The one from before, you loved her. Embers under the fire.

LÉON

I prefer the naked flame.

EMMA

Prefer—you think so?

LÉON

Far from you, I wasted two years. What have you been doing during that time? What paths have led you from the you of yesterday to the you of today?

EMMA

Why talk about it again? I seemed to live in Yonville, but in my mind I was in Paris with you.

LÉON

How was I able to leave.

EMMA

Imagine that we were in a carriage in Paris. There, eyes tired, I shut my eyes, I saw in the shadows, twisting in the wind, the flame of gas lights. At your side, I got out of carriage in front of the peristyle of a theater. Or, rather in the salons of restaurants where one sups at midnight by candle light, we mixed in the motley colored crowd of men of letters and actresses. A life above others, between heaven and earth, something sublime.

LÉON

And while you were dreaming like that I was plunged without rest in my studies, trying vainly to forget you.

EMMA

Ah, how nice it would have been to live together.

LÉON

Aren't we happy now?

EMMA

It's sure. I'm crazy. Hold me.

LÉON

The essential thing is being together, isn't it? This room in an inn—hasn't it become our room? You are going to find your pins under the base of the clock, and when you put the red conch shells by the chimney to your ear, you will hear the noise of the sea that you love to hear.

EMMA

Yes, you are right. But if you knew my sadness returning after I've left your arms! Often travelers get out of the carriage and I remain alone until we start up again. So I cry, sending you kisses that are lost in the wind. The next day, I'm dead in my soul, and I begin to count the days until your caresses.

LÉON

My beloved!

EMMA

Your caresses. And then, afterward? You will leave me, you will get married, you will do like the others.

LÉON

What others?

EMMA

Why, men! You are all infamous!

LÉON

Emma, I want to know. You haven't loved others—say? Don't laugh.

EMMA

Do you think you caught a virgin?

LÉON

No, don't laugh. Understand me and tell me the truth. Did you love someone else before me?

EMMA

Why should I lie to you? Yes, I loved someone before you. Not like you! Not like you! And don't be jealous, go! He's really nothing now.

LÉON

What did he do?

EMMA

He was a Captain in the Navy. He left and he won't come back.

LÉON

And that's why, even in our embraces, I read that sadness in the depths of your eyes.

EMMA

I love you. I love you. I love you as I can, as much as I can. But I am weary, you see, so weary! What hopes raised me in the past when I emerged from the convent, and in my father's home. I was expecting to begin to live! What freedom in the summer evening in broad light. What an abundance of illusions. Nothing more remains now. I have spent the whole of my life like a traveler leaving all his riches in the inns of the route.

LÉON

I no longer belong to myself the way I belong to you. You told me the other day I was born for your happiness. Is that no longer true?

EMMA

Yes! I want to love you! Don't budge! Don't talk, look at me! Stay put! I brought you a rose from my rose bush.

(she opens her corsage and the rose appears between her breasts)

Take it. With your mouth.

LÉON

It's your body which has perfumed it.

EMMA

Your arms! It's only in them that I still feel happiness.

LÉON

Emma.

(she has unhooked all her clothes, and holding them in one hand goes to push the bolt)

EMMA

My beloved child! Come.

(The lights dim. The Beauties appear)

BEAUTIES

When one is at the end of one's courage, it's nice to have let
oneself be loved.
If passion has bruised your soul, it's a revenge to lend your body
to pleasure.
When one discovers great things in oneself, one applies oneself
to be contented with small joys.
You weep that life has cheated you. Do you imagine that you
didn't cheat yourself?
You had heroic ambitions for virtue, the splendor of renuncia-
tion, the halo.
But you were not that woman.
And the pure love you made bloom. Behold, you're making it in
the beds of inns!
You had ambitioned the storms of the heart, the sacredness of
adventure, intoxication.
And behold you are enmeshed completely in shabby lies of
bourgeois adultery.
If the baseness of such happiness suffices you—??
Emma! Emma!
You really wouldn't be that woman?

CURTAIN

ACT III

SCENE 16

The Bovary garden.

The blue sky of a summer afternoon. The Sun excavates numerous holes through the shade of the arbor. Félicité and Justin hang linen to dry on a clothes line.

FÉLICITÉ

If you're going to stay here it's to help me pick up my work and not to stand around gaping at each skirt or kerchief! So you've never seen it, flute player! What's this chemise got? As if your lady didn't wear the like.

JUSTIN

Ah, indeed, yes! Madame Homais! She's not a woman like Madame.

FÉLICITÉ

And the hemmed pants. Is it the pride of Saint Maclou or are you looking to see if the handsome Léon hasn't forgotten something?

JUSTIN

How do you have the heart to laugh, nasty girl! I will tell Madame about the night you showed Theodore your room.

FÉLICITÉ

It would be vain to see if she dared to reproach me! Who do you think was able to hide the letter that was hidden in the basket of apricots? And then I know too many other things on her account, both green and ripe.

JUSTIN

Is it of her that you speak like that?

FÉLICITÉ

No, it's the Pope!

JUSTIN

Nasty little devil that you are!

FÉLICITÉ

And if I were to tell her that you come to cajole me to clean her boots, and you spent a whole day kissing them?

JUSTIN

That would be a falsehood.

FÉLICITÉ

For once it would make her laugh.

JUSTIN

I forbid you to tell her. I forbid you.

FÉLICITÉ

Have no fear, big ninny. I'm singing to tease you.

JUSTIN

Félicité, you must promise me.

FÉLICITÉ

Slacken the rope, fifi.

(sings)

My Ninette is just fourteen
And three months something.
Her complexion is like the Spring.
Her mouth is like the rose.

(Enter Emma)

EMMA

Send Lheureux to me right away.

FÉLICITÉ

He promised to be here on my heels.

(Félicité and Justin leave. Emma allows herself to collapse on the bench. Her negligee of imitation lace would scandalize Yonville.)

EMMA

Saturday, Sunday, Monday. Day after tomorrow, tomorrow. The day that counts.

(shrugging her shoulders)

The hour that counts. And then Friday, Saturday.

(Lheureux enters)

LHEUREUX

Your maid came to inform me that you desire to speak to me. I learn with pleasure that you are completely well again.

EMMA

Here, sir. Here's what I found yesterday evening upon returning from Rouen.

LHEUREUX (nods)

Master Hareny, bailiff of Buchy. Yes, Vincart, banker of Rouen. Yes, yes,. It's a protest. It's a protest, unfortunately.

EMMA

Well?

LHEUREUX

What can I do about it?

EMMA

You gave me your word not to circulate that note. Did you lie to me?

LHEUREUX

I agree that I promised you. But I was forced myself. I had the knife at my throat.

EMMA

And what's going to happen now?

LHEUREUX

Oh, it's very simple. A court judgment and the seizure. That's all.

EMMA

Is there no way to calm this Mr. Vincart?

LHEUREUX

Calm Vincart! Plainly, you don't know him. He's more ferocious than an Arab!

EMMA

But sit down, will you, Mr. Lheureux!—I am sure that if you wanted to—

LHEUREUX

No other way than to give him his money or at least a good part of it. Can you do it?

EMMA

No, but you yourself—

LHEUREUX

Again! A poor shop-keeper like me doesn't have the means to make advances everlastingly. I make myself ill with all the devils, with my health always so—so, and despite the current of opportunities, I don't make enough to butter my bread.

EMMA

My good Mr. Lheureux—

LHEUREUX

I don't actually know where our account stands, the loans, the furnishings, the interest, the renewals, the commissions,—it never ends. It gets me all mixed up. No, decidedly, I'm not meddling with it any further.

EMMA

That's fine. I'll address myself elsewhere.

LHEUREUX

You know quite well, Madame Bovary that if I could wheedle Vincart this morning, I didn't delude myself by employing it. If I even saw some return of funds I would put them at your disposal without hesitation. I'm round like an apple.

EMMA

What's the use of all this, since you have no money and neither do I?

LHEUREUX

You don't have cash, but you do have wealth. Yes, at Barneville, that orchard that belongs to a small farm sold by Bovary's father. It cannot bring you very much. In your place I'd get rid of it, and perhaps I'd even have a surplus.

EMMA

How much should I ask for it?

LHEUREUX

You still have the power of attorney?

EMMA

Yes, but where to find a buyer?

LHEUREUX

I'm already busy with that, and I've learned after difficult actions that a certain Langois covets the property without revealing his price.

EMMA

I will accept whatever he wants to pay.

LHEUREUX

Not at all, you must wait, take your time, sound the guy out. The thing is worth at least a trip. If you are prevented from making it, I offer to go to the place myself, to be of service to you, and to chat with this Langois.

EMMA

How much do you think I can get?

LHEUREUX

I don't know. Emough to make Vincart release his judgment.

EMMA

Then go to Barneville and do your best.

LHEUREUX

At least—

EMMA

At least?

LHEUREUX

Unless you don't prefer at the same time, I mean to say partially—the debt of Mr. Bovary.

EMMA

What debt? My husband also owes you something?

LHEUREUX

I found him in bad shape, the poor man, during your illness. He's a brave lad, although together we had difficulties—

EMMA

With him? But on what subject? He told me nothing!

LHEUREUX

On account of your first note. The one you signed to me on the day you fell ill.

EMMA

It's true. I'd forgotten about that.

LHEUREUX

It fell due—at the end of three months. I had to present it to the Doctor. You were in no condition to listen to my explanations.

EMMA

And what did he say?

LHEUREUX

At first he seemed surprised, and even more so, at the supplementary bill, that I was obliged to give him At the same time, right?

EMMA

What bill?

LHEUREUX

The travel articles.

EMMA

My God!

LHEUREUX

Then he got carried away. He insisted that you'd never ordered it, that it was not possible, that I was trying to deceive him. As for me, I defended myself as was just. There were some words. But, we made it up. He insisted that you know nothing, to keep you from all worry.

EMMA

He's never mentioned it to me.

LHEUREUX

He ended by signing a recognition, and even a few days later asked me to provide a small sum for him—fifty crowns You may imagine that I did it with pleasure.

EMMA

But, in that case, in that case,—how much do we owe you now?

LHEUREUX

I was telling you just now that I don't know myself. Besides, the expiration dates are very far away. Let's occupy ourselves with Vincart's protest for the moment, with the sale of this hovel, and not bother your head about the rest. For each day, it's pain suffices.

(Enter Homais)

HOMAIS

Ah, dear Madame. I came to seek in your peaceable dwelling a little consolation. I present my respects to you. Please excuse me, Mr. Lheuruex, for interrupting you.

LHEUREUX

Not at all, not at all. Besides, I've finished taking orders from Madame. You can count on three ells of lace for the heads of the chairs. Goodbye, Madame, and always at your service. My respects, Mr. Homais.

HOMAIS

Good evening! Good evening!

(Lheureux leaves.)

This here is the port after the storm.

EMMA

What's happened to you that's so terrible?

HOMAIS

Imagine. In my mess there's an armoire in which I lock up all the toxins, corrosives, narcotics, and putrefiers which the necessities of my profession compel me to be supplied with. They are all under lock and key, and the key's hung on a nail behind the door.

EMMA

And the key disappeared?

HOMAIS

Not at all. I ordered Justin to wash the armoire. He extracted diverse flasks, pots, glass jars, receptacles of all sorts and shapes, then after having dried the shelving put the contents back and put it in good order, adjust the hinge and give me a report that my orders had been executed.

EMMA

Nothing better.

HOMAIS

Wait! The preparation of an essence of Borage having called me into the laboratory, what did I see on my credenza? A large blue bottle sealed in yellow which contained a white powder and on which a label in my own handwriting in red ink and in gothic script—the word "Dangerous".

EMMA

Well?

HOMAIS

It's a supply of arsenic, Madame. My student had forgotten to put it back in the armoire. How, at the sight of it, I wasn't floored by a sudden apoplexy? How many funereal results might have sprung from this unforgiveable negligence! There's no poison more violent, and of more certain effect. Imagine, my poor dear wife entering the laboratory and taking some arsenic thinking it to be powdered sugar!

EMMA

But Madame Homais never enters the laboratory.

HOMAIS

It only needs to happen once. How I gave it to that young, corrupted kid; he made me run the risk of poisoning a sick person, no more, no less than going at my age to the bench of criminals, of seeing me dragged to the scaffold.

(Enter Charles accompanied by Abbé Bournisien)

CHARLES

Hello, my little pussy, how do you feel?

EMMA

Fine, fine, my friend.

CHARLES

I met the priest, and he thought, as I do, that a little sweet cider wouldn't do us any harm in this heat.

EMMA

Hello, Father Bournisien.

BOURNISIEN

Yes, I accepted without manners—coming to drink to your

complete recovery.

CHARLES

Hello, Mr. Homais.

BOURNISIEN

I didn't see you there in the shadows. Hello, Mr. Homais.

HOMAIS

Hello, Mr. Bournisien.

CHARLES

I told Félicité in passing to get the cider so as not to disturb you.

HOMAIS (to Emma)

Silence before the clergy if you please. It would be annoying if the story of this incident spread through the vestries.

CHARLES

Tell me. It's really a young Miss Lempereur who gives you lessons?

EMMA

Yes.

CHARLES

Well, I recently was at the home of Madame Liegeard, and saw a lady by that name who professes the piano. I mentioned you to her, and she swore to me she doesn't know you.

EMMA

How is that possible? She must have forgotten my name.

CHARLES

I thought that at Rouen there might be several Misses Lempereur, mistresses of the piano.

EMMA

Perhaps. I'll go through my receipts to see if her first name is on the bills.

CHARLES

Oh, that's not necessary. Imagine that my wife insisted on having rusty fingers, and assured me that lessons were necessary from the best professor. I hesitated a bit all the same. Twenty francs per lesson when the ladies of Mercy only charge fifty sous. But Emma certified that I understood nothing and I had to accept.

HOMAIS

You did well to make up your mind. You must never leave the faculties of nature uncultivated.

BOURNISIEN

The Holy Evangelist teaches us that.

HOMAIS

The Evangelist contains something of that sort.

BOURNISIEN

Sure. The parable of the talents.

CHARLES

She's made astonishing progress since she's been going there every week. Aren't you, my pretty little pussy?

EMMA

Skip it! I'm going to see about your cider.

CHARLES

But I told you that—

(Emma is gone. The men spring up.)

Don't be difficult about putting yourselves at ease. I give the example.

HOMAIS

That's not to be refused.

(Charles and Homais remove their coats. Bournisien unbuttons his frock.)

Well, Mr. Bournisien, it seems we're going to have a railroad from Rouen to Paris. The paper speaks of it as a thing decided. What does the Church say?

BOURNISIEN

Will it be as comfortable as they pretend?

HOMAIS

Think of it. The stage coaches of Lafitte and Caillard travel three miles per hour when not heavily loaded. We are assured that on the new rails the speed will reach eight miles per hour.

BOURNISIEN

Eight miles per hour. Is that possible?

CHARLES

At such a pace you won't be able to distinguish the landscapes.

HOMAIS

In less than seven hours we'll be transported from the Rue de la Grosse-Horloge to the boulevards of Paris.

BOURNISIEN

How many accidents there will be to deplore, no question! In what concerns myself, I won't risk my life going in carriages at such a mad speed. You mustn't tempt God.

HOMAIS

So you admit that religion, faithful to its secular weakness remains hostile to all progress?

BOURNISIEN

I didn't say anything like that.

HOMAIS

You are preparing to wither the railroad the way you condemned Galileo.

BOURNISIEN

Excuse me!

HOMAIS

England and the United States of America already possess vast networks of rails, exploited by locomotive machines of considerable power.

BOURNISIEN

Truly? So it's a question in that case of Protestant inventions?

HOMAIS

Who cares? You shan't stop Progress in its march. Like it or not, Mr. Bournisien, the future belongs to science. I congratulate myself on being born in this enlightened century.

(Félicité brings the cider.)

CHARLES

Here's the cider! Attention!

(he uncorks the bottle)

BOURNISIEN

How your grove is agreeable to brave the summer heat.

HOMAIS

It's true that the orientation of your garden assures you the double advantage of the air plus the breeze from the river and the rays of the rising sun.

CHARLES

Yes, we are fine here.

BOURNISIEN

You've got everything you need to be happy.

HOMAIS

Take care of pushing the cork with prudence, as the liquid, saturated as it is with specific acid risks splashing in your face.

BOURNISIEN

It's goodness would leap to your eyes.

(All approve with heavy laughter, and expand into seats, glasses in hand.)

CURTAIN

ACT III
SCENE 17

A low-class orchestra ruins the air of the waltz, degraded by trombone fantasies and a cornetist.

When it stops the dirty light of a winter dawn lights the room in the Hotel of the Emperors. The door is kicked open Emma leans on the door jamb. She wears pants of black velour, and a red-silk blouse like Garvani's whores. Léon follows her wearing a large straw hat, a false nose, and a wig. Both are a little drunk.

EMMA

Like a girl! You treated me like a girl! To dare to make me dine with those creatures. Did you actually hear their laughs.

(she imitates their laughter)

LÉON

What's to be done? A night of Lent? It was my friends who brought them you know. And besides, you didn't have to come.

EMMA

I was thirsty. I jumped all night. Hop! Did you see they made a circle around me? All twisted, masks, quadrilles, lights of chandeliers, all, all, all!

LÉON

Your shitfaced!

EMMA

The smell of punch in that restaurant. What a restaurant! You couldn't find one more mediocre and less expensive. No?

LÉON

You don't worry yourself about money, like an archduchess.

EMMA

Don't complain. Don't I pay the surplus expenses when we are together? As for you, you only think about pinching pennies. As for me, I always need something around us. Something that resembles luxury. Look, rather! The Hotel of the Emperors!

(she bursts into laughter)

LÉON

There are people sleeping.

EMMA

That's why this week I sold my little vermillion spoons, the last thing that I had to sell and that I stole from my husband.

(she laughs)

LÉON

Shut up, will you?

EMMA

Don't talk that way, bourgeois that you are! Banal, avaricious more than a woman. Love is as flat as marriage.

LÉON

There are moments that you scare me.

EMMA

Horrify you, too? No?

LÉON

Yes. When you clasp me against your icy body, your naked arms around me, face covered with cold drops, and lips which stammer. I have before me, yes, your immense eyeballs. And they don't see me.

EMMA

You should run away. What keeps you?

LÉON

I love you.

EMMA

Are you sure of it?

LÉON

Very sure. My mother has received letters, she wrote me, she had my boss talk to me. They invoked my position, my future, showed me the abyss into which I was sliding—and I had to swear never to see you again.

EMMA

You waited to be drunk to tell me.

LÉON

But while I was swearing, I knew I wouldn't keep my word.

EMMA

You regret it?

LÉON

Yes, I don't admit that you consume me the way you do. Each day more. I promise myself to revolt, to free myself, to force myself to cherish you less. The crack of your boots in the corridor and my will is gone.

EMMA

Like an alcoholic before the bottle.

LÉON

That's it.

EMMA

Then slide into the abyss. So much the worse for you. It's been a long while that I've weighed you, judged you. Well before, no question, having confessed my deception to myself. But it pleased me to go to it furiously again, to extract pleasure from you. When love is no more, pleasure remains. Has there ever been love?

LÉON

I adored you.

EMMA

To dream, desire, attain. And what I touch in the end is already no more than rottenness between my fingers. Life doesn't suffice to hope. Each joy calls a new disgust. The best kisses only leave on the lips desire for another sensuality.

LÉON

You know quite well I'm ready to be damned with you and that nothing can tear us apart.

EMMA

I no longer want to live, or rather to sleep, to sleep.

LÉON

You know quite well that I love you.

EMMA

Don't blaspheme. Will it ever come that the one who says to me these words is not lying? The man to whom I could not lie. He would be strong. He would be handsome. He would know how to command me.

(knocking at the door)

JUSTIN'S VOICE

Madame, are you there, Madame?

(Emma opens the door)

EMMA

You, Justin! What is it?

JUSTIN

I came with a deed. Yesterday, at night, they placed yellow placards over your door and on the pillars of the market.

EMMA

What placards?

JUSTIN

To announce the seizure and the sale of your furniture.

EMMA

The gall.

JUSTIN

Yes, Madame! I tore the placards down as soon as they turned their backs! I waited until everyone was asleep, and then I got a horse from the stable at the Lion d'or, and galloped to find you. Mr. Bovary saw nothing. Nobody but Félicité. You must come right away.

EMMA

Yes, yes, I must. I will go find Lheureux. Perhaps he only wants to scare me. Wait for me downstairs. I'll join you. We'll leave.

JUSTIN

Right away, Madame.

(she tears off her costume and dresses during what follows.)

LÉON

I don't understand what's happening.

EMMA

Why, yes, you understand quite well. I have TO FIND MONEY. Right away. Ten thousand francs.

LÉON

You are exaggerating the danger. I am sure that a thousand will quiet your good fellow.

EMMA

No, this time it's no longer true. I feel that Lheureux is trying to frighten me. I don't even know the amount. Eight thousand at least.

LÉON

How could I obtain that amount?

EMMA

Try. Would you prefer to allow me to be sold? I really don't know anything. You could get a loan yourself, promise yourself, or bring your guarantee.

LÉON

No, no—it's impossible on account of my mother. But my friend Morel, the son of the ship owner should be back in two or three days. He's very rich. He won't refuse at least a portion.

EMMA

But Léon, it's not in three days, it's now I need the money. In three days it will be too late.

LÉON

It's useless for me to consider—

EMMA

Try! Try! Try! My darling, you will see how I will love you.

LÉON

You cannot find eight thousand francs just like that.

EMMA

But if I was in your shoes I would know quite well how to find them.

LÉON

Where's that?

EMMA

In your study.

LÉON

What do you mean?

EMMA

Didn't you just tell me that you were ready to damn yourself for me?

LÉON

Emma!

EMMA

Léon! And that nothing could tear us apart? Prove it! You told me it was you who keep the cash box for the study.

LÉON

You want to make me a thief?

EMMA

Big words! As if you had to steal! It's a question of an advance for a few days since this money is needed right away. Understand, will you! As soon as I have found it, you'll put it back in the cash box.

LÉON

I haven't got the right—

EMMA

Nobody will ever know. You are going to save me, my love. I am yours. I will be yours better still.

LÉON

Leave me alone. Get out of here.

(she starts to leave)

Emma!

EMMA

My darling.

(but he hangs his head)

LÉON

I'm an honest man.

EMMA

Coward!

(she flees.)

CURTAIN

ACT III
SCENE 18

The back room of Lheureux's shop.

Black desk, straw chairs.

Lheureux is writing in a large register. Emma enters.

EMMA

Mr. Lheureux.

LHEUREUX

Servant! I'll be with you.

(he continues to write.)

EMMA

Mr. Lheureux, I am in a hurry.

LHEUREUX

Me, too, Madame; an urgent matter. A moment's patience if you
please.

(A long pause. Lheureux closes his register.)

Well?

EMMA

You know what's happening to me. It's a joke, right?

LHEUREUX

No, it's not a joke.

EMMA

But, still—

LHEUREUX

Did you think, little lady, that I was going to be your supplier and banker for the King of Prussia until the end of time? I have to go back into my disbursements. Let's be fair.

EMMA

I have just read your papers. It's impossible that I owe you such a sum.

LHEUREUX

The Court recognized it.

EMMA

Your bills, your loans, even with all the interest, and all the commissions that you will—we are far from that sum.

LHEUREUX

There's a judgment. They showed it to you. Seizure follows judgment in legal postponement. Anyway, it's not me, it's Vincart. I've returned all my credit to him.

EMMA

You couldn't—?

LHEUREUX

Nothing at all! It would be easy, certainly. Each time one wanted a bauble—you'd only have to order old man Lheureux, and he will bring it to you straight away. You lack money to amuse yourself? Who doesn't have it, Papa Lheureux was there right away, very honored to be at the orders of the princess. And then the time comes all the same, the end of the end, to pay the score. "Couldn't you—?" Then pay good Papa Lheureux with smiles.

EMMA

Let's discuss it, will you? It's a surprise. If I had been able to anticipate it, I would have taken measures, I would have thought what to do.

LHEUREUX

You received the summons in plenty of time.

EMMA

Your blue papers! Your grey papers! I don't understand them at all. I didn't even read them. So, I am not prepared.

LHEUREUX

Whose fault is it? While I am at the stake, like a Negro, you spend your time having fun.

EMMA

Moralizing.

LHEUREUX

Over the price. That never injures.

EMMA

Mr. Lheureux, I beg you, you must have pity.

LHEUREUX

Are you trying to seduce me?

EMMA

Wretch!

LHEUREUX

Ha, ha. How you do go on!

EMMA

I will make known what you are. I will tell my husband.

LHEUREUX

Who's preventing you? What could he do, given that the law is on my side? And between ourselves, do you think that I would have nothing to apprise him of—on my side!

EMMA

Wretch!

LHEUREUX

Again? Look, look. A seizure is not amusing, I know it. I went through it when I was young, and I promised myself, that henceforth, I would do the seizing. But, after all, one doesn't die of it. And it's the only way I have of forcing you to find my money.

EMMA

But where will I find it?

LHEUREUX

When one has friends like you do—

EMMA

I don't understand.

LHEUREUX

Then why are you turning pale?

(A long pause. Lheureux reopens his register and starts to write.)

EMMA

I will sign.

LHEUREUX

I've already had enough of your signatures—too much.

EMMA

I will sell again.

LHEUREUX

What? You no longer have anything to sell. Excuse me, I have to work.

EMMA

How much cash is needed to stop all actions?

LHEUREUX

It's too late.

EMMA

But if I were to bring you several thousand francs?

LHEUREUX

No.

EMMA

A quarter of the sum?

LHEUREUX

No.

EMMA

A third?

LHEUREUX

No.

EMMA

Almost all?

LHEUREUX

It's useless. Goodbye, Madame.

EMMA

I entreat you, Mr. Lheureux. A few days more.

LHEUREUX

I don't have time to waste.

C U R T A I N

ACT III
SCENE 19

The garden.

Winter has despoiled the trees of their leaves, making the sky a gray skeleton where naked branches of Wisteria stand tall. On the bench, dead leaves end by rotting.

Justin watches.

JUSTIN

Félicité! Félicité! Here's Madame.

(Emma enters, Félicité rushes in)

FÉLICITÉ

Madame! Madame! Don't go in the house. The Bailiff is there with two men. It's an abomination. They are going through everything. They've counted all the plates in my kitchen. Do I really have to let them do it?

EMMA

There's nothing more to let them do.

FÉLICITÉ

The poor Doctor who left to see his patients without suspecting
a thing.

EMMA

The poor Doctor.

FÉLICITÉ

And Lheureux? You've seen him? Well?

EMMA

Nothing to expect! Nothing more.

FÉLICITÉ

But Madame, it's not possible!

EMMA

You see plainly it is.

FÉLICITÉ

But you must look about, speak to people.

EMMA

What's the use?

FÉLICITÉ

Mr. Guillaumin? If I were you, I'd go to him.

EMMA

Why?

FÉLICITÉ

You would do well to go there.

EMMA

You think?

FÉLICITÉ

Theodore has often told me when speaking of you, how pretty he found you. If you would only take the trouble—

EMMA

I am to be pitied, but not to be sold—

FÉLICITÉ

Ah—Mr. Boulanger?

EMMA

Rodolphe! Even less. Never—

FÉLICITÉ

If he was at La Hachette—

EMMA

Luckily, he probably isn't at La Hachette.

FÉLICITÉ

Mr. Tuvache? Mr. Binet?

EMMA

It's useless. Go find the bailiff.

FÉLICITÉ

Why, there's really no one?

EMMA

There's no one. Go.

(Félicité leaves)

JUSTIN

I am here.

EMMA

What could you do for me, my poor Justin?

JUSTIN

Whatever is necessary. I would steal. I would kill.

EMMA

You would dare to steal for me?

JUSTIN

You have only to tell me.

EMMA

You wouldn't be cowardly?

JUSTIN

I don't want you to lose your lace, your nice smells, and the cloth of your blouses, to be like others. I don't want them to take your little slippers, nor your andirons where you lean your feet, nor the cushion at the back of your arm chair in which the crease of your head remains noticeable for a moment when you leave it. What you have touched, no one must touch.

EMMA

You, Justin?

JUSTIN

I prefer to protect you, and if I cannot save you, I would love, at least, to die for you.

EMMA

You are a child!

JUSTIN

But the others, who are men, are they asking to die?

(Emma lowers her head in silence)

Pardon me; I didn't say anything. I have nothing to say. I don't permit myself. Whatever makes you happy, you are right to do it. Forgive me, Madame! Use me. Whatever you order me, I will obey you.

EMMA

You've been so close, right here. It's funny.

JUSTIN

Don't make fun!

(a long pause)

EMMA

Justin, Justin. Will you do what I ask?

JUSTIN

Yes.

EMMA

Whatever it may be?

JUSTIN

Whatever it may be.

EMMA

In Mr. Homais' laboratory, in the armoire, the famous armoire— you know there's a flask containing a powder, a white powder.

JUSTIN

I know. Arsenic.

EMMA

You are going to go there, without being seen, and bring me back a full fistful.

JUSTIN

Why?

EMMA

I need it.

JUSTIN

But, Madame—

EMMA

You're afraid!

JUSTIN

No.

EMMA

You already refuse to obey me.

JUSTIN

No. But it's a poison, a poison.

EMMA

And if I wanted to rid myself of someone? Wouldn't you agree to help me, to be my accomplice? Someone who has always done me harm?

JUSTIN

I will go.

EMMA

Right away. Be careful that no one sees you. I am waiting for you. A full fistful. Go, quick!

(Justin leaves)

And all the same it was love.

(Félicité appears.)

FÉLICITÉ

Madame, The Doctor's here. He only asked if you were here, and he went in to his office as usual. He had his head like every day. Probably, he didn't notice the poster. He doesn't know yet. But he will find out from the Bailiff, from one minute to the next. What's he going to do?

EMMA

He'll take a long time to understand, and after that he'll cry a lot, wiping up his sobs and hiccups.

FÉLICITÉ

It would be better if you went to tell him yourself.

EMMA

Tell him what? "The rug you walk on is no longer yours, you have no furniture in your house, not a needle, and I'm the one who's ruined you, because I was cheating on you."

FÉLICITÉ

Maybe he'll find a way of straightening things out. He will forgive you.

EMMA

For sure he would forgive me! Who knows that he wouldn't ask my forgiveness.

FÉLICITÉ

He's so good.

EMMA

Yes, he would be good, generous, magnanimous. Exactly what I don't want.

FÉLICITÉ

But what are you hoping for then?

EMMA

A way to arrange things myself.

FÉLICITÉ

Truly?

EMMA

You will see. Wait till he knows. Seize the moment. He will cry. He will call me. Tell him I left, and persuade him to go meet me. He's got to leave.

FÉLICITÉ

That will be easy.

EMMA

I will wait here.

FÉLICITÉ

You aren't cold?

EMMA

Not yet.

(Félicité leaves. Emma is shaken by a great tremor.)

The cold.

(A long silence Justin enters)

You have it?

JUSTIN

Yes.

EMMA

No one saw you?

JUSTIN

No.

EMMA

Give me Your full handful. That's fine.

(She grasps the arsenic in her right hand.)

JUSTIN

What are you going to do now?

EMMA

Don't worry. Dust your hand carefully. Would you like to kiss me for your trouble?

JUSTIN

Ah, Madame!

(She's the one who kisses his mouth. He lays his head on Emma's knees.)

CHARLES' VOICE

Emma! My wife.

(Justin raises his head. She places his head back with her left hand and hides his head in her skirt.)

EMMA

Don't worry, I tell you.

CHARLES' VOICE

Emma!

(she opens her hand and greedily eats the arsenic. Charles' voice extinguishes in a sob.)

Emma!

EMMA

Is it really true that you love me?

JUSTIN

Why do you ask me that?

EMMA

So you will tell me.

JUSTIN

I don't know what to say.

EMMA

I would like to hear that. I've been cherished, above all, without limit, like no one else in the world. I would like so much to hear it.

JUSTIN

I don't know what to say.

EMMA

By a love greater than life, by a love—

JUSTIN

What's wrong with you? Madame? Madame!

EMMA

It's nothing. I'm going to go in now. No one must know that you came.

JUSTIN

How you are trembling!

EMMA

It's nothing. It's the cold.

CURTAIN

ACT III
SCENE 20

The Beauties reappear.

BEAUTIES

Appeasement.
Redemption.
Silence.
Because deceptions shorten your life.
Virtue!
Passion!
Pleasure!
Who else could you seek refuge with, except she who does not
    deceive?
Life only lies to you.
Death always keeps its promises.
You will no longer have anything to covet.
You will no longer have the trouble of betraying.
It is well to choose one's time.
Push the door.
Cross over the sill.
Reject the burden.

(In the penumbra, a lamp flickers in Emma's room. Charles,
Homais and Félicité agitate around the bed as Emma agonizes.)

FÉLICITÉ

A napkin! On the chest of drawers.

HOMAIS

Doesn't it seem indicated to you to attempt an analysis of her excrement?

CHARLES

Whatever you like. Save her, my friend! I don't know any more. I don't know anything.

FÉLICITÉ

The traces of blue on her face.

CHARLES

My God, my god! Why didn't you say something?

EMMA

I'm thirsty.

HOMAIS

Sensation of dryness in the pharynx.

FÉLICITÉ

Here it is.

CHARLES

Here, drink.

HOMAIS

Still she's purged. I would dare to employ the word "superpur-
gation," and from the moment the cause ceases, the effect must
cease, in good logic.

(Charles sobs at the foot of the bed.)

EMMA

Don't cry. Soon, I will no longer torment you.

CHARLES

I didn't know you were unhappy. Is this my fault? I did what I
was capable of.

EMMA

I hurt! Ah.

THE BEAUTIES

Don't cry!
Don't seem to suffer.
Let there be nothing ugly in your last gesture.
Let there be nothing vulgar in your last word.
You must ruin yourself nobly—in the shadows.

EMMA

I'm burning! I'm burning!

HOMAIS

Intolerable pain in the epigastus.

FÉLICITÉ

The basin. She's going to start vomiting again.

HOMAIS

We should be able to attempt some tapping if we dispose of the instrument, *ad hoc*.

EMMA

Don't touch me! Don't touch me!

CHARLES

I am not capable of anything.

FÉLICITÉ

She cannot vomit because her teeth won't stop clapping.

EMMA

I have a fire in my belly.

THE BEAUTIES

Deceitful right to the end.
She doesn't know how to die in beauty.

(The Beauties withdraw.)

FÉLICITÉ

Should I go for a priest?

CHARLES

Yes, yes. Go.

HOMAIS

Perhaps, it's a salutary paroxysm. It's not yet certain that we ought to despair. One of our masters, the illustrious Cadet de Gassicourt reports cases wherein, after the most powerful antidotes have been tried in vain—

EMMA

A mirror.

(Charles brings a mirror and holds it in front of her. She sits up and passes her hand over her face, and tries to hum the tune of the waltz as tears run down her cheeks. Then she bursts out in a desperate laugh and suddenly falls back.)

CHARLES

Emma! Emma!

(Silence. Everything extinguishes slowly. In the shadows, the organ resumes the waltz, muted at first, then more amply and more gravely. The room reappears. Emma, dead, is stretched on the bed in her wedding gown, with white satin slippers, a crown, a big veil. The light of candles flicker on her face with waxen blue lips and eyes closed. Bournisien and Homais watch her, but they are dozing.)

HOMAIS (starting up)

Listen!

(Bournisien opens his eyes.)

Do you hear a dog howling?

BOURNISIEN

They pretend they smell death. It's the same with bees. They fly from the hive of deceased persons.

HOMAIS

What unqualifiable superstition! Nevertheless, the noise that animals make at such times does have the effect of shaking the nerves, especially when one is, as I am, worn out with fatigue, and whose sensibility is over-excited.

BOURNISIEN

Are you trying to say in that way that you are afraid?

HOMAIS

Me, afraid? I've seen many others when I studied pharmacy. And I even intend to bequeath my body to hospitals so as to serve science until the very end. Nothingness doesn't shock a philosopher.

BOURNISIEN

It's to blaspheme without shame that you interrupted my prayers!

HOMAIS

You mean your sleep. Because you were snoring loudly and I was re-reading Voltaire.

BOURNISIEN

You are an impious person, Mr. Homais!

HOMAIS

You are an ignorant person, Mr. Bournisien.

BOURNISIEN

Take a break, all the same, it will dissipate.

(They doze off. Enter Charles who remains standing, face to face with the dead.)

CHARLES

Emma! My Emma! I've just found the letters. I have you there for the last night in our wedding cloths, and I've just read the letters of your lovers. Without a doubt, it's my fault. I loved you. I didn't understand you. Who were you, really?

(Emma appears before the room where her body remains stretched.)

EMMA

A poor woman.

CHARLES (neither sees nor hears)

All the same, the best of my life.

(Charles weeps, motionless before the bed. The Beauties appear and surround Emma.)

THE BEAUTIES

Emma, come with us.
For us, too, there's a great distance between dream and reality.
From words to things.
From what one thinks to be and what one is.
But it mustn't be admitted, except on this side here.
Come share our secret.
Come with us to ensnare others.

EMMA

I am not worthy.

THE BEAUTIES

Imagine tomorrow,
Instead of ruminating over today.
Not to desire impossible joys
To prefer very safe roadsteads
To a great shipwreck!

EMMA

All that I did was mediocre.

THE BEAUTIES

Yes, but you weren't satisfied with it.

EMMA

I didn't give true happiness to anyone.

THE BEAUTIES

Yes, but you didn't consent to yours.

EMMA

I squandered my life.

THE BEAUTIES

Yes, but you didn't accept it.

(The Beauties take Emma by the hand and pull her away.

The organ music increases and plays the waltz.)

C U R T A I N

ABOUT THE AUTHOR

Frank J. Morlock has written and translated many plays since retiring from the legal profession in 1992. His translations have also appeared on Project Gutenberg, the Alexandre Dumas Père web page, Literature in the Age of Napoléon, Infinite Artistries. com, and Munsey's (formerly Blackmask). In 2006 he received an award from the North American Jules Verne Society for his translations of Verne's plays. He lives and works in México.

www.ingramcontent.com/pod-product-compliance
Lightning Source LLC
Chambersburg PA
CBHW022014090426
42739CB00006BA/133